I0448665

BIOWATCH: LESSONS LEARNED AND THE PATH FORWARD

HEARING

BEFORE THE

SUBCOMMITTEE ON EMERGENCY PREPAREDNESS, RESPONSE, AND COMMUNICATIONS

OF THE

COMMITTEE ON HOMELAND SECURITY HOUSE OF REPRESENTATIVES

ONE HUNDRED THIRTEENTH CONGRESS

SECOND SESSION

JUNE 10, 2014

Serial No. 113–70

Printed for the use of the Committee on Homeland Security

Available via the World Wide Web: http://www.gpo.gov/fdsys/

U.S. GOVERNMENT PRINTING OFFICE

90–880 PDF   WASHINGTON : 2014

For sale by the Superintendent of Documents, U.S. Government Printing Office
Internet: bookstore.gpo.gov   Phone: toll free (866) 512–1800; DC area (202) 512–1800
Fax: (202) 512–2250   Mail: Stop SSOP, Washington, DC 20402–0001

COMMITTEE ON HOMELAND SECURITY

MICHAEL T. MCCAUL, Texas, *Chairman*

LAMAR SMITH, Texas
PETER T. KING, New York
MIKE ROGERS, Alabama
PAUL C. BROUN, Georgia
CANDICE S. MILLER, Michigan, *Vice Chair*
PATRICK MEEHAN, Pennsylvania
JEFF DUNCAN, South Carolina
TOM MARINO, Pennsylvania
JASON CHAFFETZ, Utah
STEVEN M. PALAZZO, Mississippi
LOU BARLETTA, Pennsylvania
RICHARD HUDSON, North Carolina
STEVE DAINES, Montana
SUSAN W. BROOKS, Indiana
SCOTT PERRY, Pennsylvania
MARK SANFORD, South Carolina
VACANCY

BENNIE G. THOMPSON, Mississippi
LORETTA SANCHEZ, California
SHEILA JACKSON LEE, Texas
YVETTE D. CLARKE, New York
BRIAN HIGGINS, New York
CEDRIC L. RICHMOND, Louisiana
WILLIAM R. KEATING, Massachusetts
RON BARBER, Arizona
DONALD M. PAYNE, JR., New Jersey
BETO O'ROURKE, Texas
FILEMON VELA, Texas
ERIC SWALWELL, California
VACANCY
VACANCY

BRENDAN P. SHIELDS, *Staff Director*
MICHAEL GEFFROY, *Deputy Staff Director/Chief Counsel*
MICHAEL S. TWINCHEK, *Chief Clerk*
I. LANIER AVANT, *Minority Staff Director*

———————

SUBCOMMITTEE ON EMERGENCY PREPAREDNESS, RESPONSE, AND COMMUNICATIONS

SUSAN W. BROOKS, Indiana, *Chairwoman*

PETER T. KING, New York
STEVEN M. PALAZZO, Mississippi, *Vice Chair*
SCOTT PERRY, Pennsylvania
MARK SANFORD, South Carolina
MICHAEL T. MCCAUL, Texas *(ex officio)*

DONALD M. PAYNE, JR., New Jersey
YVETTE D. CLARKE, New York
BRIAN HIGGINS, New York
BENNIE G. THOMPSON, Mississippi *(ex officio)*

ERIC B. HEIGHBERGER, *Subcommittee Staff Director*
DEBORAH JORDAN, *Subcommittee Clerk*

CONTENTS

BIOWATCH: LESSONS LEARNED AND THE PATH FORWARD

Tuesday, June 10, 2014

U.S. HOUSE OF REPRESENTATIVES,
SUBCOMMITTEE ON EMERGENCY PREPAREDNESS,
RESPONSE, AND COMMUNICATIONS,
COMMITTEE ON HOMELAND SECURITY,
Washington, DC.

The subcommittee met, pursuant to call, at 10:03 a.m., in Room 311, Cannon House Office Building, Hon. Susan W. Brooks [Chairwoman of the subcommittee] presiding.

Present: Representatives Brooks, Palazzo, Sanford, and Payne.

Mrs. BROOKS. Good morning. The Subcommittee on Emergency Preparedness, Response, and Communications will come to order. The subcommittee is meeting today to receive testimony regarding the Department of Homeland Security's BioWatch program.

The BioWatch program was established in 2003 in the aftermath of the anthrax attacks that killed 5 people and sickened more than 20 others. The program is a system of detectors deployed to more than 30 U.S. cities to scan for a number of aerosolized biothreat agents.

Recognizing the limitations of the current system, in 2008 the Department's Office of Health Affairs began the process to acquire a next-generation detector known as Gen–3. After a series of missteps spanning two administrations, 6 years, and millions of dollars later, Secretary Johnson recently canceled that acquisition on April 29, 2014.

We know through the subcommittee's biothreat hearing in February and a subsequent Classified briefing that the threat of bioterrorism is real. In fact, in its BioWatch analysis of alternatives performed for the Department, the Institute for Defense Analyses noted that the bioterrorism threat has not changed since 2001.

With that in mind, robust biosurveillance and biodetection capabilities are vital to our country's security. I am interested in hearing from Dr. Brinsfield and Dr. Brothers about their efforts to work together going forward to develop, test, and deploy a next-generation technology.

I am also interested in learning more about efforts to enhance the currently deployed system to make it more effective as we await new technology, and about the Department's overall biosecurity strategy.

In July 2012, the administration released its National Strategy for Biosurveillance. This strategy was supposed to be followed 120 days later by an implementation plan. However, nearly 2 years later, that plan has still not yet been completed.

This is simply unacceptable. I hope our witnesses will be able to shed some light on the administration's strategy and when that implementation plan will be complete.

As we consider what is next for BioWatch, we must be mindful of what went wrong with Gen–3 so we learn from those mistakes. Unfortunately, this is not the first failed acquisition in the Department's history.

SBInet and others have suffered from management shortcomings, be they requirement settings or a failure to follow proper acquisition protocols, such as the completion of alternatives analyses or cost-benefit analyses.

We can't afford to waste a single dollar of Homeland Security funding. I am interested in hearing from Secretary Cummiskey on the Department's efforts to mature its acquisition system and oversight of large-scale acquisitions, such as Gen–3.

It is my hope that the acquisition legislation introduced by my colleague, Mr. Duncan of South Carolina, which the House just passed yesterday, will help to strengthen the Department's acquisitions management capabilities.

With that, I look forward to hearing from our distinguished panel of witnesses and to continuing the subcommittee's examination of the bioterrorism threat facing our country, and our programs and capabilities to address that threat.

The Chairman now recognizes the gentleman from New Jersey, Mr. Payne, for any opening statement he may have.

[The statement of Chairwoman Brooks follows:]

JUNE 10, 2014

STATEMENT OF CHAIRWOMAN SUSAN W. BROOKS

The BioWatch program was established in 2003 in the aftermath of the anthrax attacks that killed 5 people and sickened more than 20 others. The program is a system of detectors deployed to more than 30 U.S. cities to scan for a number of aerosolized biothreat agents.

Recognizing the limitations of the current system, in 2008 the Department's Office of Health Affairs began the process to acquire a next generation detector, known as Gen–3. After a series of missteps spanning two administrations, 6 years, and millions of dollars later, Secretary Johnson cancelled that acquisition on April 29, 2014.

We know, through this subcommittee's biothreat hearing in February and a subsequent Classified briefing, that the threat of bioterrorism is real. In fact, in its BioWatch analysis of alternatives performed for the Department, the Institute for Defense Analysis noted that the bioterrorism threat has not changed since 2001.

With that in mind, robust biosurveillance and biodetection capabilities are vital to our security. I am interested in hearing from Dr. Brinsfield and Dr. Brothers about their efforts to work together going forward to develop, test, and deploy a next generation technology.

I am also interested in learning more about efforts to enhance the currently deployed system to make it more effective as we await new technology and about the Department's overall biosecurity strategy.

In July 2012, the administration released its National Strategy for Biosurveillance. This strategy was supposed to be followed, 120 days later, by an implementation plan. Nearly 2 years later, that plan has still not been completed. This is simply unacceptable. I hope our witnesses will be able to shed some light on the administration's strategy and when that implementation plan will be complete.

As we consider what is next for BioWatch, we must be mindful of what went wrong with Gen–3 so we learn from those mistakes. Unfortunately, this is not the first failed acquisition in the Department's history. SBI–Net, the A–S–P program, e-Merge, and TASC all suffered from management shortcomings, be it requirements setting, or a failure to follow proper acquisition protocols, such as the completion of alternatives analyses or cost benefit analyses.

We cannot afford to waste a single dollar of security funding. I am interested in hearing from Secretary Cummiskey about the Department's efforts to mature its acquisitions system and oversight of large-scale acquisitions, such as Gen–3. It is my hope that the acquisitions legislation introduced by my colleague, Mr. Duncan of South Carolina, which the House passed just last night, will help to strengthen the Department's acquisitions management capabilities.

With that, I look forward hearing from our distinguished panel of witnesses and to continuing the subcommittee's examination of the bioterrorism threat and our programs and capabilities to address it.

Mr. PAYNE. Good morning. I would like to thank Chairwoman Brooks for holding today's hearing on the cancellation of BioWatch Gen–3 acquisition and the future of biosurveillance and detection.

The Department of Homeland Security's decision to cancel the BioWatch Gen–3 acquisition raises several questions, but I think they can be boiled down to two.

First, if Gen–3 is canceled, what are we going to do instead? Second, with about $100 million already appropriated to the canceled Gen–3 acquisition, what efforts is DHS undertaking to make sure that acquisition decisions are made more responsibly in the future?

To the first question, I understand that the current budgetary constraints contributed significantly to the Department's decision to cancel the Gen–3 acquisition. I appreciate DHS's efforts to reconcile the findings of the analysis of alternatives, BioWatch detection goals, and existing fiscal limitations.

I trust that the Secretary's decision, though difficult, was informed, thoughtful, and deliberate.

But the threat posed by biological weapons remains.

In February, as stated, this subcommittee held a hearing on bioterrorism and each witness had the same message—the threat posed by biological weapons still exists, and the consequences of such an attack would be devastating if we could not identify and quickly respond.

Accordingly, I would be interested to know what and how DHS will ensure that it is maximizing the limited resources to ensure that our biodetection and surveillance capabilities address the threats identified by the intelligence community.

Turning to the broader acquisition issue, I note that in addition to serving as Ranking Member on this panel, I sit on the Subcommittee on Oversight and Management Efficiency. Over the past year-and-a-half, that panel has devoted a significant amount of time to overseeing DHS's efforts to improve acquisition management, which has been on the Government Accountability Office's high-risk list since 2005.

Although I understand that some progress has been made to get acquisition management off the high-risk list, it continues to remain to be a challenge.

Indeed, the acquisition process for BioWatch Gen–3 embodied many of the problems that plagued previous acquisitions—cost overruns, delayed deployment, and insufficient documentation to support the investment.

I commend DHS for obtaining a thorough analysis of alternatives and other preliminary acquisition documents, and for using those documents to assess the future of Gen–3.

That said, I am concerned that those foundational documents were not completed until 7 years after the BioWatch Gen–3 acquisition process began.

I would be interested to learn from the Department how it will use the lessons learned from the BioWatch Gen–3 acquisition to strengthen its acquisition policies.

I thank the witnesses for being here today and I look forward to your testimony. With that, Madam Chairwoman, I yield back the balance of my time.

[The statement of Ranking Member Payne follows:]

STATEMENT OF RANKING MEMBER DONALD M. PAYNE, JR.

JUNE 10, 2014

The Department of Homeland Security's decision to cancel the BioWatch Gen–3 acquisition raises several questions, but I think that they can be boiled down to two. First, if Gen–3 is canceled, what are we going to do instead? Second, with about $100 million already appropriated to the cancelled Gen–3 acquisition, what efforts is DHS undertaking to make sure that acquisition decisions are made more responsibly in the future?

To the first question, I understand that current budgetary constraints contributed significantly to the Department's decision to cancel the Gen–3 acquisition. I appreciate DHS's efforts to reconcile the findings of the Analysis of Alternatives, biodetection goals, and existing fiscal limitations. And I trust that the Secretary's decision—though difficult—was informed, thoughtful, and deliberate.

But the threat posed by biological weapons remains. In February, this subcommittee held a hearing on bioterrorism. Each witness had the same message: The threat posed by biological weapons still exists and the consequences of such an attack would be devastating if we cannot identify it quickly and respond.

Accordingly, I will be interested to know what how DHS will ensure that it is maximizing limited resources to ensure that our biodetection and surveillance capabilities address the threats identified by the intelligence community.

Turning to the broader acquisition issue, I note that in addition to serving as Ranking Member on this panel, I sit on the Subcommittee on Oversight and Management Efficiency. Over the past year-and-a-half, that panel has devoted a significant amount of time to overseeing DHS' efforts to improve acquisition management, which has been on the Government Accountability Office's High-Risk List since 2005. Although I understand that some progress has been made to get acquisition management off the High-Risk List, it continues to remain a challenge.

Indeed, the acquisition process for BioWatch Gen–3 embodied many of the problems that plagued previous acquisitions: Cost overruns, delayed deployment, and insufficient documentation to support the investment. I commend DHS for obtaining a thorough Analysis of Alternatives and other preliminary acquisition documents and for using those documents to inform the future of Gen–3.

That said, I am concerned that those foundational documents were not completed until nearly 7 years after the BioWatch Gen–3 acquisition process began. I will be interested to learn from the Department how it will use the lessons learned from the BioWatch Gen–3 acquisition to strengthen its acquisition policies.

Mrs. BROOKS. Thank you.

Other Members are reminded that statements may be submitted for the record.

[The statement of Ranking Member Thompson follows:]

STATEMENT OF RANKING MEMBER BENNIE G. THOMPSON

JUNE 10, 2014

Nearly 2 years ago, this subcommittee held a hearing on acquisition failures that occurred as the Department of Homeland Security pursued BioWatch Gen–3. In addition to the problems with acquisition practices, Gen–3 was wrought with cost-overruns and technical challenges at the time.

Accordingly, at that hearing, Members of this panel urged DHS to suspend acquisition activities until it completed and assessed foundational acquisition documents per the recommendations of the Government Accountability Office.

I am pleased that the Department heeded the advice of the GAO and our Members. The Department's action resulted in the completion of a thorough Analysis of Alternatives, and the time necessary to process the findings and determine the best path forward. Given the challenges the Department has experienced with acquisitions in the past, I have consistently urged it to suspend acquisition immediately when problems exist so it can re-evaluate.

I commend the Department for doing that here. Although nearly $100 million has already been appropriated to Gen–3, the Department's decision to slow down and act deliberately will save taxpayer dollars in the long-run.

That said, I echo concerns made by other members of this panel about the timing of the Analysis of Alternatives. I was also troubled to learn that there may have been alternative biodetection technologies used by other Federal agencies at the time acquisition for Gen–3 began, but it does not appear that DHS considered adapting those technologies instead of spending millions to develop its own.

I will be interested in learning whether DHS will consider biodetection technology currently used by other Federal agencies or other off-the-shelf technologies.

I am also interested in learning more about the status of currently-deployed BioWatch technology, and any challenges it faces. For example, I understand that much of the air sample and laboratory equipment may be reaching the end of their life cycle, and that some of the diagnostic technology is outdated.

How will DHS address those issues, and does it have the resources to carry out the system upgrades necessary to keep existing BioWatch technology working?

Finally, I understand that the Department is contemplating changes to the Bioterrorism Risk Assessment (BTRA). I am interested in understanding more about the changes to the BTRA, and how the Department will make sure that whatever biodetection technology is deployed addresses the threat posed.

Mrs. BROOKS. We are very pleased to have a very distinguished panel before us today and want to thank you all for your time in preparing your written testimony and for your time before us today on this very important topic.

To our left, on the panel, is Dr. Kathryn Brinsfield, serving as the acting assistant secretary of health affairs and chief medical officer for the Department of Homeland Security's Office of Health Affairs.

She began her service with DHS in July 2008, and previously served as associate chief medical officer and director of the division of workforce health and medical support within OHA.

Prior to serving as acting assistant secretary and chief medical officer, she served on a detail to the National security staff as the director of medical preparedness policy.

Before joining DHS, Dr. Brinsfield worked for various organizations, including Boston's Emergency Services, Boston Metropolitan Medical Response System, and the DelValle Emergency Preparedness Training Institute.

She graduated with honors from Brown University and received her M.D. from Tufts School of Medicine and her master's in public health from Boston University. She completed her residency in emergency medicine at Cook County Hospital in Chicago and her EMS fellowship at Boston EMS.

Our next witness is Dr. Reginald Brothers. Dr. Brothers was confirmed by the U.S. Senate on April 7, 2014, for the position of under secretary for science and technology at the U.S. Department of Homeland Security.

Prior to joining DHS, Dr. Brothers served in the U.S. Department of Defense's office of the assistant secretary of defense for research and engineering as the deputy assistant secretary of defense for research.

Dr. Brothers received a B.S. in electrical engineering from Tufts University, an M.S. in electrical engineering from Southern Methodist University, and a Ph.D. in electrical engineering and computer science from MIT.

Next is Mr. Chris Cummiskey, who was appointed acting under secretary for management at DHS in February 2014.

Prior to assuming this position, Mr. Cummiskey served as the deputy under secretary for management from May 2010 to September 2013 and earlier as the chief of staff for the Management Directorate from March 2009 until May 2010.

Prior to joining DHS, Mr. Cummiskey served as the chief information officer for the State of Arizona.

Mr. Chris Currie is an acting director in GAO's homeland security and justice team where he leads the agency's work on emergency management and National preparedness issues.

Prior to this assignment, Mr. Currie was an acting director in GAO's defense capabilities and management team where he led reviews of DOD programs.

In the decade since DHS was created, Mr. Currie has led numerous audits and assessments of DHS programs including those related to transportation security, research, and development of new technologies and the Department's efforts to test and evaluate large acquisition programs and technologies.

Mr. Currie joined GAO in 2002 and has a master's in public administration from Georgia State and a B.A. in history from the University of Georgia.

Dr. Deena Disraelly—did I pronounce that correctly—is a research staff member at the Institute for Defense Analyses. She has more than 17 years' experience conducting analysis in the chemical, biological, radiological, and nuclear realm and working in and training others to support emergency response.

Her work has focused on the policy, technological, operational, and organizational aspects of preparedness, emergency response, and consequence management, particularly as related to CBRN.

Most recently, she has been focused on working with all levels of government to develop and evaluate biological preparedness plans, technologies and activities, improving interagency collaborations, developing new CBRN medical modelling methodologies, and studying potential methods for improving emergency response and disaster management.

Dr. Disraelly joined IDA after 8 years in the Navy as a surface worker officer and Naval nuclear engineering officer. Additionally she served as a researcher for 2 years at MIT's Center for Transportation and Logistics.

I must say, this is one of the most incredible panels that we have had to address the subject at hand and we are very, very pleased that you all could be with us today.

Your full written statements will appear in the record, and I will now recognize Dr. Brinsfield for 5 minutes.

As you know, the light is green, it will become yellow when you have 1 minute and if you—when the light becomes red, if you could please come close to wrapping up, we would appreciate it so we can make sure we hear from everyone.

As you also may know, other Members will be coming in and out before the panel due to other commitments with other hearings.

So with that, Dr. Brinsfield for 5 minutes.

STATEMENT OF KATHRYN BRINSFIELD, ACTING ASSISTANT SECRETARY, OFFICE OF HEALTH AFFAIRS, U.S. DEPARTMENT OF HOMELAND SECURITY

Dr. BRINSFIELD. Thank you, ma'am.

Chairman Brooks, Ranking Member Payne, and distinguished Members of the subcommittee, thank you for inviting me to speak today. I appreciate the opportunity to testify on biological defense and specifically the BioWatch Program.

I am honored to testify alongside my colleagues, Dr. Brothers and Mr. Cummiskey, as well as our colleagues from the GAO and IDA.

As this is my first appearance before this subcommittee, please allow me to provide an overview of the Office of Health Affairs and the responsibilities of the chief medical officer of the Department of Homeland Security.

OHA provides health and medical expertise in support of the DHA mission to prepare for, respond to, and recover from all threats. Our mission is to advise, promote, integrate, and enable a safe and secure workforce and Nation in pursuit of National health security.

The chief medical officer is the principle medical adviser to the Secretary and to DHA components for all health security matters, including those having a CBRN nexus, and has a statutory responsibility to lead coordination of the Department's biodefense activities.

To that end, OHA conducts policy, planning, and operations related to preparing for and ensuring rapid response to biological events whether naturally-occurring, such as a pandemic, or man-made, such as an intentional release of aerosolized anthrax.

Effective management of risks from biological threats and hazards depends on early warning and shared situational awareness. So critical decisions surrounding response and recovery are timely, well-informed, and ultimately save lives.

The National Biosurveillance Integration Center, or NBIC, is housed with OHA and has the key responsibility to integrate, analyze, and share the Nation's biosurveillance information to advance the safety, security, and resilience of the Nation. As a 24/7 operation, NBIC uses information technology tools that assist the collaborative process of integrating information and expertise bound to cross its biosurveillance partners at all levels of government.

Just as surveillance is critical, detecting a biological attack early and identifying the biological agent is an essential part of our multi-layered approach to biodefense. The BioWatch Program was initially fielded in 2003 within 33 days of its announcement at President Bush's State of the Union address and has been operational 24 hours a day, 365 days a year for more than 10 years.

The program is a Nation-wide biosurveillance and detection system intended to partner with State and local public health and responder communities to enhance our Nation's ability to respond to a bioterrorism event.

The sampling technology used by the BioWatch Program is designed to detect the intentional catastrophic release of select aerosolized biological agents and has a robust quality assurance element that includes laboratory and field audits to ensure accuracy.

BioWatch has proven itself a key component of the Nation's biodefense architecture. However this technology must be improved in response to the evolving threat in a cost-effective manner.

In 2008, the BioWatch Program began examining new technologies to streamline operational timeliness, increase coverage and decrease costs. BioWatch began a technology acquisition known as Gen–3 to provide autonomous detection capability generating results as soon as 4 to 6 hours after the release of a biological agent rather than 12 to 36 hours needed by current operations.

In 2012, the Government Accountability Office conducted a review of the acquisition and recommended that BioWatch perform an analysis of alternatives or AOA to ensure that BioWatch pursue an optimal solution.

Using this recommendation, OHA requested that the Institute of Defense Analysis conduct an independent AOA to include a market survey of available biodetection technologies and a cost-benefit analysis. The purpose of the AOA in this process was not to issue a specific recommendation but to help inform DHS's decision to proceed with any acquisition of biodetection technology.

It was our assessment that the AOA suggested that an autonomous detection capability would be a valuable addition to current BioWatch operations in certain circumstances. However it did not find an overwhelming benefit to justify the cost of a full technology switch including one-to-one replacement and expanded coverage within and to new jurisdictions.

Following a thorough review of the acquisition of record, the AOA and other studies on the future of biodetection capabilities, OHA, in consultation with our DHS colleagues, concluded that the autonomous detection system under consideration would not meet program objectives and recommend that the DHS leadership cancel its acquisition. This decision was formalized in an acquisition decision memo on April 29, 2014.

Cancellation of the Gen–3 acquisition in no way lessens the importance of BioWatch current operations or the need to explore advancement in biodetection capabilities. OHA and S&T are now completing a plan to both test currently-available technology solutions and to look at indoor and outdoor applications.

I want to emphasize that the Secretary, the Department, and our offices remain committed to the BioWatch program, its role in a layered-approach biodefense, and the advancement of its technological capabilities.

Thank you, and I look forward to answering your questions.

[The joint prepared statement of Dr. Brinsfield and Mr. Brothers follows:]

9

JOINT PREPARED STATEMENT OF KATHRYN BRINSFIELD AND REGINALD BROTHERS

JUNE 10, 2014

Chairman Brooks, Ranking Member Payne, and distinguished Members of the subcommittee, thank you for inviting us to speak with you today. We appreciate the opportunity to testify on biological defense and specifically the Department of Homeland Security's BioWatch program. We're honored to testify alongside Acting Under Secretary Cummiskey as well as our colleagues from the Government Accountability Office (GAO) and the Institute for Defense Analysis (IDA).

THE BIOTERROR THREAT

More than a decade after anthrax was mailed to Members of Congress and to media organizations, dozens of policy, intelligence, and technical reports have affirmed the viability of terrorist groups and violent extremists using biological weapons to cause death, suffering, and socio-economic disruption on a calamitous scale. In 2008, the Congressional Commission on the Prevention of Weapons of Mass Destruction Proliferation and Terrorism stressed the near-term and growing threat that terrorist use of biological weapons pose. The DHS Office of Health Affairs (OHA) and the Science and Technology Directorate (S&T) have worked diligently to increase understanding of the full spectrum of potential threats and their consequences as well as countermeasures and means of prevention.

In 2001, the Defense Science Board affirmed that "there are no technical barriers to a large-scale bioattack." We are living in the midst of a biotechnology revolution in which the knowledge and tools needed to acquire and disseminate a biological weapon are increasingly accessible. It is possible today to manipulate pathogens' characteristics (e.g., virulence, antibiotic resistance) and even to synthesize viruses from scratch. These procedures will inexorably become simpler and more available across the globe as technology continues to mature. Thankfully, the combination of technical expertise required and the restrictions limiting the acquisition of the materials necessary for production still make this a challenging task.

Even small-scale attacks, however, could be highly lethal and disruptive, and as has been noted, there is a real possibility of a campaign of bioattacks on multiple targets (the "reload" phenomenon)—because some of these weapons are self-replicating organisms. Moreover, it is not necessary for a nation-state to maintain a large stockpile of bioweapons as the development of a significant offensive bioattack capability could occur within weeks or months.

Biological threats, including bioterrorism, pandemics, emerging infectious diseases, and animal and plant diseases, remain a top homeland security risk. A biological attack could impact any sector of our society and would place enormous burdens on our Nation's public health, security, and critical infrastructures. The 2014 Quadrennial Homeland Security Review includes a review of the biological threat landscape and the Department's strategy to counter these threats. One aspect of our overarching strategy includes robust biosurveillance capabilities that provide situational awareness and early detection. These capabilities are important because in a biological event, every moment counts. The faster we detect an event, the faster we can take life-saving steps such as providing medical countermeasures and containing the threat.

BIOSURVEILLANCE

It is challenging to recognize early indications of a biological attack because its release is invisible, and because of the global availability of pathogenic organisms, the dual-use nature of the required materials, and the small operational footprint necessary to produce the agents. Advance detection and disruption of a bio-weapons program will continue to be difficult and, as such, cannot be relied upon as the main focus of U.S. defenses against biological attacks. Instead, the United States has made a deliberate strategic choice to detect an attack through bio-agent release detection technology programs such as BioWatch and mitigate its affects by enhancing the capabilities of first responders and public health professionals to detect bio-agents in the field and conduct reliable lab analyses. Other investments to improve our early detection capability include working to create sensors capable of automatically initiating protective actions (e.g., altering a building's airflow patterns) and developing rapid diagnostic capabilities to guide our response.

Effective management of biological threats and hazards depends on early warning and shared situational awareness, which in turn support response and recovery decision making that is timely, well-informed, and ultimately saves lives. The United States has numerous biosurveillance capabilities across human health, plant, animal, food, water, and environmental domains distributed broadly across Federal, State, Tribal, territorial, and local government and the private sector. The National Biosurveillance Integration Center (NBIC), operated through the DHS Office of Health Affairs (OHA), is the designated Government entity charged with integration, analysis, and dissemination of the Nation's biosurveillance information in order to advance National safety, security, and resilience.

NBIC is a 24/7 operation that collaborates daily with the BioWatch program as well as other National Biosurveillance Integration System (NBIS) Federal department and agency partners and State, local, Tribal, and territorial entities. At this time, NBIC is monitoring and reporting on, among other biological events, avian influenza H7N9 in China; Middle East Respiratory Syndrome Coronavirus (MERS-CoV) in a number of countries now including the United States; Chikungunya Fever in the Caribbean; Ebola Virus Disease in West Africa; and the highly pathogenic avian influenza H5N1 world-wide.

BIOLOGICAL DETECTION AND THE BIOWATCH PROGRAM

Early detection of a biological attack and identification of the biological agent involved are critical to containing the spread of the agent as well as the successful treatment of affected populations. Early detection is part of a multi-layered approach to providing public health decision makers more time—and thereby more options—in responding to, mitigating, and recovering from a bioterrorist event or other threat to public health. If release of a bioagent is detected and assessed in a timely fashion, an appropriate prophylactic treatment can be started prior to the widespread onset of symptoms resulting in more lives saved.

BioWatch is the only civilian-managed, Nation-wide surveillance and detection system for aerosol biological releases, and it is intended as an interface for State and local public health and responder communities to jointly respond to a bioterrorism event. The sampling technology used by the BioWatch program is designed to detect the intentional catastrophic release of the most threatening aerosolized biological agents. The BioWatch system consists of units that collect air samples in more than 30 cities and a network of local, State, and Federal laboratories that analyze samples on a daily basis with a goal of providing warning of possible biological attacks within 12 to 36 hours of an agent's release. The BioWatch program has a robust quality assurance element that includes laboratory and field audits to ensure accuracy. BioWatch has conducted 37 laboratory and 20 field audits to date. For more than 10 years, BioWatch has operated 24 hours a day, 365 days a year. It is a proven asset to the Nation's overarching biodefense architecture.

The initial deployment of BioWatch in 2003 was intended to provide the most comprehensive detection network possible within budgetary, time, logistical, operational, and technical constraints. The complex coordination required to achieve the successful rollout of BioWatch across a broad range of Government and private entities was a difficult and hard-earned achievement. The BioWatch program was designed to be able to advance its technological capabilities to meet an evolving threat. Although technology can always be improved, the challenge is to do so cost-effectively and in pace with the evolving threat.

AUTONOMOUS DETECTION ACQUISITION ACTIVITIES

As the *National Strategy for Biosurveillance* states, we must foster innovation and facilitate new biosurveillance activities—including new detection technologies. In 2008, as directed by Congress, the BioWatch program began examining new technologies to shorten operational timelines, increase coverage, and decrease costs. Acknowledging the benefit of early warning of a biological attack and the prompt distribution of medical countermeasures, the program began exploring technologies that could reduce detection and response times in a cost-effective manner.

For this reason, BioWatch began a technology acquisition process—known as Generation 3, or Gen–3—to provide autonomous detection capability that would eliminate the time-consuming steps of collecting filters by hand and transporting them to a laboratory for analysis. An autonomous detector is designed to be a "lab-in-a-box" where the sampling and analysis processes will take place within the device, generating results as soon as 4 to 6 hours after the release of a biological agent, rather than the 12 to 36 hours needed by current operations. The BioWatch program began a phased acquisition for automated detection technology. Phase I was completed in June 2011 and assessed the maturity and technical capability of the biodetection technology market against a robust set of system requirements. These requirements included technical assay/characterization testing of two candidate systems and limited field testing of one vendor's candidate autonomous detection system.

In September 2012, the Government Accountability Office (GAO) recommended that BioWatch perform an Analysis of Alternatives (AoA) as well as re-evaluate its mission needs statement to ensure acquisition requirements were well-grounded and that the BioWatch program was pursuing an optimal and cost-effective solution. In an Acquisition Decision Memorandum issued September 7, 2012, the Acquisition Decision Authority (ADA) directed the BioWatch program to prepare a solicitation/request for proposal (RFP) for an AoA study, consistent with GAO's recommendation.

The AoA study, conducted by the Institute for Defense Analysis, was concluded on August 30, 2013, and the final report was released on December 20, 2013. Following an exhaustive market survey, the AoA report analyzed four different methodologies, not favoring one over another. The intent of the AoA was not to issue a recommendation but to help inform DHS's decision to proceed with any acquisition of BioWatch technology.

CANCELLATION OF GEN–3 ACQUISITION

The AoA determined that an autonomous detection capability would be a valuable addition to current BioWatch operations. However, it did not find an overwhelming benefit to justify the cost of a full technology switch (one-to-one replacement and expanded coverage within jurisdictions). Following a thorough review of the Gen–3 acquisition of record, the AoA and other studies on future biodetection technology, OHA, in consultation with S&T, the Management Directorate, and the Office of Policy, concluded that the autonomous detection system under consideration would not meet program objectives at a reasonable cost and recommended that DHS leadership cancel its acquisition. Secretary Johnson then directed Acting Under Secretary for Management Cummiskey to cancel the BioWatch Gen–3 technology acquisition. In accordance with this guidance, and per the Department's Management Directive 102 on acquisition procedures and processes, Acting Under Secretary Cummiskey convened the Acquisition Review Board for the BioWatch Gen–3 acquisition to formally cancel the acquisition of record on April 24, 2014. This cancellation reflects the need to implement cost-effective solutions, as it is critical that any upgrades to the technology be acquired and deployed in a staged manner and in parallel—not in place of—the current operational program.

THE PATH FORWARD

Cancellation of the Gen–3 acquisition of record in no way reduces the capability of existing BioWatch operations or the need to investigate potential advancements in biodetection capabilities. OHA and S&T are working closely on the development of a systems approach to next-generation biodetection, including joint development of requirements moving forward. Evaluation of the existing operational BioWatch system is underway and will guide near- and long-term investments in new or updated capabilities. A full range of potential investments is under consideration from near-term incremental improvements to longer-term shifts such as a distributed, networked, sensor-agnostic biosurveillance architecture currently under development at S&T with potential for capability well beyond what the Department initially envisioned for Gen–3.

Using newly-delegated prize authority,[1] S&T and OHA have a platform for engaging and harvesting non-traditional Government performers through a biosurveillance grand challenge on this issue of National importance. S&T is also exploring a "Beyond BioWatch" Apex Lite[2] program that will, in partnership with OHA and other National biodefense stakeholders, work toward implementation of an integrated National systems approach to biodetection. We would be happy to share this vision and strategic approach to biosurveillance research with the subcommittee as it takes shape in the near future.

---

[1] The America Creating Opportunities to Meaningfully Promote Excellence in Technology, Education, and Science Reauthorization Act of 2010 (America COMPETES Reauthorization Act Pub. L. 111–358) outlines authorities for all Federal agencies to conduct prize competitions to engage broadly the American public to stimulate innovation that may potentially advance their agency mission.

[2] Apex projects are cross-cutting, multi-disciplinary efforts requested by DHS components that are high-priority, high-value, and short turn-around in nature. They are intended to solve problems of strategic operational importance identified by a component leader. Apex Lite projects will be a middle ground between traditionally-managed projects and Apex efforts, building off lessons learned from previous Apex projects and scaling critical Apex elements to different time lines, scopes, and foci.

CONCLUSION

We want to emphasize that the Secretary, the Department, and our offices remain committed to the operational BioWatch Program, the role of vigilant biosurveillance as part of the layered approach to the Nation's biodefense, and the advancement of innovative technological capability as part of an integrated systems approach to surveillance. In the coming years, we intend to focus our limited developmental resources on capacities to detect bioattacks in near-real time in order to enhance protective response actions. However, we will also have to consider future needs for detection of a wider range of potential threat agents, including genetically-altered, synthetic, or unanticipated agents, and possibly to enable detection of food and surface contamination. Faster, more detailed, and more reliable characterization of bioevents will be necessary to improve situational awareness and inform response. We must continue to develop an agile approach that accommodates possible epidemics of emerging disease or attacks using unforeseen bioagents or agents not addressed by stockpiled countermeasures. Strategies for coping with and stopping bioterror campaigns must be developed. Mechanisms of international cooperation in dealing with infectious disease outbreaks and collaborative approaches to financing and refining needed biodefense technologies and countermeasures must evolve.

OHA and S&T are committed to working together with our colleagues across the interagency to address these challenges. We are deeply appreciative for this subcommittee's continued support for our shared goals of health and homeland security.

Mrs. BROOKS. Thank you. The Chairwoman will now recognize Dr. Brothers for 5 minutes.

STATEMENT OF REGINALD BROTHERS, UNDER SECRETARY, SCIENCE AND TECHNOLOGY DIRECTORATE, U.S. DEPARTMENT OF HOMELAND SECURITY

Mr. BROTHERS. Thank you, Chairman Brooks, Ranking Member Payne, and distinguished Members of the subcommittee. Thank you for the opportunity to join you today to discuss the Science and Technology Directorate, lessons learned from the BioWatch acquisition and the Department's unified approach to biosurveillance moving forward.

It is a privilege to appear before you today, along with my DHS colleagues from health affairs and the management directorate, as well as distinguished experts from the GAO and IDA.

Today, science and technology were once drivers of threats and sources of solutions for those threats have also improved the lives of countless people. Take the internet, for one example. By connecting people and facilitating the flow of information, it is a central driver of the modern economy. It is also, among other things, a platform of choice for distributing IED recipes, has made communities around the world vulnerable to potentially devastating cyber attacks.

With numerous potential industrial, environmental, and human impacts, biotechnology and the evolution of modern biosciences have a potential to be the next major disruptive force along the lines of the information technology revolution.

Already, the availability of equipment and information has broken down barriers previously insurmountable to individuals outside State-funded biological programs. That means that the risk of groups or individuals creating and using a powerful bioweapon is real.

Since becoming under secretary for science and technology, I have seen first-hand a passion at S&T for work on these types of tough problems. It really is a passion. Walking the halls of the directorate, I hear how excited people are to get up in the morning and put their shoulder into tough homeland security problems.

For addressing biological risks to homeland security, we work hand-in-hand with a broadly-based community of biodefense professionals and stakeholders, to develop technology that enables better preparation for and more effective response to biological attacks.

At S&T, our National Biodefense Analysis and Countermeasures Center in Fort Detrick, Maryland is a fully integrated element of our Nation's biodefense and National resource retribution and analysis during bioterrorism or biocrime events. Our chemical and biological defense division is dedicated to providing comprehensive biological threat characterization, as well as development of capabilities for pre-event assessment, discovery, and interdiction and for warning, notification, and analysis during incidents.

As you know, the BioWatch program was once a part of the directorate. S&T has a long history of research and development support to the BioWatch program from before DHS's Office of Health Affairs or OHA was created through the present time.

In my time at S&T, I have seen a very functional, a very positive working relationship with OHA. We are unified in pursuit of the shared goal of development and implementation from an effective and efficient National biosurveillance framework. That is encouraging to me. Because now more than ever, S&T and OHA must be totally synchronized. The cancellation of BioWatch Gen–3 acquisition gives us at DHS an opportunity to jointly evaluate the current operational BioWatch program and to offer systems approach to next-generation biodetection.

Numerous lessons learned by S&T, OHA and management directorate, are already guiding our unified path forward; for that reason, creating positive relationships between all three of our organizations. I am confident that we won't repeat past mistakes.

Moving forward, S&T and OHA will evaluate the full range of near- and long-term investments in new or updated capabilities. This includes potential for short-term, incremental improvements to the existing BioWatch system. This also includes longer-term shifts toward a distributed, networked, sensor-agnostic architecture with potential capability well beyond what the Department initially envisioned for the Gen–3 acquisition.

At S&T, we are considering a potential BioWatch Apex program, Beyond BioWatch Apex program. Like other Apexes, this would be cross-cutting multidisciplinary effort and be focused on high-priority problems and would have a leadership buy-in in robust partnership between organizations.

It would, in partnership with OHA and other National buyer defense stakeholders, work toward implementation of integrated National systems approach to biodetection. As part of this effort, we also look forward to using newly available tools like prize authority. These have potentials of platform for biosurveillance grand challenge that would allow S&T and OHA to access untapped energy, enthusiasm, expertise from the broader community of Government performance.

As I am sure my colleagues will all agree, I believe all the ingredients necessary for a unified path forward for joining implementation of long-term vision for biosurveillance will make Americans safe at a reasonable cost are in place at DHS. Working together, S&T and OHS, OHA's energetic workforces have the expertise and experience necessary to successfully develop a technology that will be a pillar for our Nation's next-generation biodefense.

We certainly learned from lessons in the past, but we are focused right now on the opportunity before us to make a lasting impact on the Nation's long-term biodefense and the opportunity to safeguard the country against current emerging biological threats.

To close, I want to thank you again for the opportunity to join today's discussion. The ingredients for success are in place, and we at DHS are unified in our path forward.

I look forward to your questions.

Mrs. BROOKS. Thank you. The Chairwoman now recognizes Mr. Cummiskey for 5 minutes.

STATEMENT OF CHRIS CUMMISKEY, ACTING UNDER SECRETARY, MANAGEMENT DIRECTORATE, U.S. DEPARTMENT OF HOMELAND SECURITY

Mr. CUMMISKEY. Thank you.

Good morning, Chairman Brooks, Ranking Member Payne, Congressman Palazzo. Thank you for the opportunity to appear before you today to discuss lessons learned from the BioWatch program, as well as specifically discussing the acquisition of Generation–3. I also want to thank my fellow colleagues, the DHS, as well as the GAO, and the Institute for Defense Analysis for their dedicated work in this important area.

As you understand the under secretary for management is also the chief acquisition officer for the Department. I oversee the policies and procedures used to acquire and oversee over $18 billion in goods and services each year. During my tenure, I have focused significant attention on improving the analysis and rigor for all phases of the acquisition life cycle.

During the past 5 years, DHS has continued to focus on strengthening our acquisition oversight policies to ensure our major programs are steeped in established management principles. As indicated by GAO, we have made substantial progress in building an oversight process with clear and logical approval of gateposts backed by business intelligence that flags programs that are off-track.

I am pleased to report that in the past 3 years, no program has been authorized to proceed to the next Acquisition gatepost, unless they have followed the rigor prescribed in our governing policy, Management Directive 102, which was put into place in 2010.

The BioWatch program has played an important role in the Department's layered approach to mitigate new and evolving threats in providing Nation-wide biosurveillance capability. BioWatch Gen–2 has successfully monitored selected aerosolized biothreat agents in highly-populated areas.

I want to reaffirm the Secretary's commitment to Generation–2 as the Department's program of record for aerosol biological threat detection. In 2009, Congress authorized the Department to begin the development and testing of Generation–3 and noted that DHS must strike a careful balance between expediting the deployment of new technologies and ensuring that such technologies be fully validated.

The Department, now through MD–102 requires clear and cogent planning documents that are closely tracked throughout the acquisition life cycle.

In September 2012, GAO concluded that the performance, schedule, and cost expectations presented in the early estimates were not developed with the rigor required in MD–102. As a result, significant adjustments were made to both schedule and cost estimates.

GAO further recommended that BioWatch perform an analysis of alternatives or AOA, as well as reevaluate the mission needs statement to ensure acquisition requirements were well-grounded.

In an acquisitions decision memorandum issued in September of that same month, then-Under Secretary for Management Rafael Borras, as the chief acquisition officer, paused further development of the BioWatch Gen–3 program pending the findings of the AOA.

In December 2013, the AOA was published and found that while an autonomous detection capability would be a valuable addition to current BioWatch operations, there was not an overwhelming benefit to justify the cost of a full technological replacement estimated at $5.7 billion.

Following a thorough review of the Generation–3 acquisition of record, the AOA and other studies of future biotechnology detection, Department officials concluded that the autonomous detection system under consideration would not meet the program's objectives.

Based on this information, Secretary Johnson tasked me to take the appropriate actions to cancel all acquisition-related activities associated with BioWatch Gen–3.

On April 24, I convened an acquisition review board and directed that the Science and Technology Directorate work in concert with the Office of Health Affairs BioWatch program office to explore the development of an effective and affordable automated aerosol biodetection capability going forward.

In conclusion, DHS has worked diligently to improve its acquisition processes and these efforts have produced more effective governance to current and future acquisitions.

BioWatch is an example of the relevant application of the Department's improved acquisition oversight process.

As the Department's chief acquisition officer, I can assure you this morning that I will continue to evaluate the risks of this program and will only provide authorization to proceed when well-established criteria are met.

Thank you, Madam Chairwoman.

[The prepared statement of Mr. Cummiskey follows:]

PREPARED STATEMENT OF CHRIS CUMMISKEY

JUNE 10, 2014

Chairwoman Brooks, Ranking Member Payne, and other distinguished Members of the subcommittee, I thank you for the opportunity to appear before you today to discuss lessons learned from the BioWatch program, specifically with regard to acquisition of Generation–3.

I wish to express appreciation to my colleagues from the Government Accountability Office (GAO) for their long-standing and dedicated work to support the transformation of management at DHS. Over the past 4 years, we have forged an excellent working relationship and reached common ground on many issues. I am gratified by their recent comments that recognized the substantial progress the Department has made to address its high-risk areas. We are committed to sustaining that progress given the concrete changes we've made to solidify our acquisition management infrastructure, which includes policies, delegations, business intelligence, and governance.

As Chief Acquisition Officer, I oversee the policies, processes, and procedures used to acquire and oversee over $18 billion in goods and services each year. During my tenure, I have focused significant attention on improving the analysis and rigor for all phases of the acquisition life cycle, from the requirements-development phase through implementation. This includes applying a more disciplined approach and greater vigor in the detailed analysis required before authorizing programs to proceed to the next phase of the life cycle.

When I arrived at DHS nearly 5 years ago, the Management Directorate was in the process of strengthening acquisition policies and procedures. Former Under Secretary Rafael Borras and I directed our program management oversight function to ensure that any new procedures adhered to established management principles, and balanced risk mitigation with the need for rapid deployment. Our goal was to build an oversight process with clear and logical approval "gate posts" and business intelligence that could "flag" programs that were off-track. Finally, we wanted risk to be a significant factor considered during all acquisition decision events especially at the planning phase when strategies are developed. While the preference is to seek "existing" technologies, I understand that the Department's mission may sometimes require development of higher-risk, emerging technology.

I am pleased to report that in the past 3 years, no program has been authorized by the Acquisition Review Board (ARB) to proceed to the next acquisition phase unless it has completed the required reviews and documentation.

BACKGROUND

In 2011, Under Secretary Borras and I created the Office of Program Accountability and Risk Management (PARM) to serve as the Department's central oversight body for major acquisition programs. A few of PARM's principal oversight responsibilities is to standardize policy, conduct independent assessments of major programs at each stage of the life cycle, and ensure those programs have sufficient documentation before requesting authorization from the ARB to proceed to the next phase.

To further drive common processes and procedures, Management Directive (MD) 102–01 was issued to serve as the Department-wide policy for acquisition programs and is recognized by all component executives as the road map to document and manage their programs. In recent years, the ARB has increased its oversight reach and has taken action to cancel or pause several poor-performing/higher-risk programs that were not achieving the pre-established cost, schedule, and performance goals. When a program is paused, the DHS chief acquisition officer conducts an assessment and if the program should continue forward with development, the lead program manager develops the appropriate acquisition strategy and path forward. The program will remain in paused status until the chief acquisition officer approves the acquisition strategy and path forward.

In accordance with this directive, acquisition decisions are made throughout a program's life cycle based on valid cost estimates and planning documents, such as Mission Needs Statements and Operational Requirements Documents. In the past 4 years, the Department has made great strides to improve the governance and oversight of acquisition programs. The oversight framework has been further strengthened through the establishment of a Component Acquisition Executive structure that serves as the single point of accountability for programs within the components. I rely heavily on the CAEs to support PARM by providing day-to-day oversight of major programs within their components.

Since 2009, not only have we have forged a comprehensive integration strategy, we have also demonstrated substantial progress, which led GAO to acknowledge in their 2013 High-Risk report that, "Significant progress has been made to transform and integrate the Department into a more cohesive unit." In fact, they stated in December 2012 that, "the Department has made substantial progress in many areas and if their Integrated Strategy is fully implemented, they are on a path to be removed from the High-Risk List." Any progress we have made is the direct result of an across-the-board commitment by operational components and support components to follow a clear and logical strategy. This progress has been reinforced by the willingness of our components and line-of-business chiefs to leverage best practices in both the procurement and program management disciplines.

In April of this year, Secretary Johnson issued a memorandum directing the Department to further unify its efforts in the way we plan, program, budget, and execute our investments. One of the principal focus areas of the Unity of Effort initiative is the continued refinement of our acquisition oversight framework, especially in the earliest stages where acquisition requirements are developed.

BIOWATCH PROGRAM

The BioWatch program plays an important role in the Department's layered approach to mitigate new and evolving threats by providing Nation-wide biosurveillance capability. BioWatch Generation–2 (Gen–2) is successfully monitoring for select aerosolized biothreat agents in highly-populated areas. I want to reaffirm the Secretary's commitment to Gen–2 as the Department's program of record for aerosolized biological agent threat detection.

In 2009, Congress authorized the Department to begin the acquisition of a next generation (Generation–3, or Gen–3) BioWatch system that would be able to respond autonomously to the aerosol release of certain biothreat agents, providing significantly earlier detection than Gen–2 and enabling quicker deployment of life-saving medical countermeasures. Congress noted that DHS must "strike a careful balance between expediting the deployment of new technologies and ensuring that such technologies have been fully validated." Congress appropriated $34.5 million for field testing of systems beyond Gen–2 and requested that any resulting contracts be awarded competitively. It is important to note that acquisitions of new or emerging technology pose a higher risk than traditional acquisitions given the need to field cost-effective solutions at a pace that matches the evolving threat. As such, the Department requires clear and cogent planning documents that are closely tracked and followed throughout the development life cycle.

In September 2012, GAO concluded that the performance, schedule, and cost expectations for the Gen–3 acquisition, which predated the issuance of MD–102, were not developed with the rigor required in that document. As a result, significant adjustments were made over time to both schedule and cost estimates. GAO further recommended that BioWatch perform an Analysis of Alternatives (AoA), as well as re-evaluate its mission needs statement to ensure acquisition requirements were well-grounded and that BioWatch pursued an optimal solution. In an Acquisition Decision Memorandum issued September 7, 2012, the Under Secretary for Management, as the Acquisition Decision Authority, directed the BioWatch program to develop requirements and conduct an AoA.

In December 2013, the AoA was published and found that an autonomous detection capability would be a valuable addition to current BioWatch operations. However, it did not find an overwhelming benefit to justify the cost of a full technology replacement. Following a thorough review of the Gen–3 acquisition of record, the AoA, and other studies on the future biodetection technology, the Office of Health Affairs, in consultation with the Science & Technology Directorate, Office of Policy, and Management Directorate, concluded that the autonomous detection system under consideration would not meet program objectives and recommended that DHS leadership cancel its acquisition.

Based on this information, Secretary Johnson directed me to cancel all acquisition-related activities associated with BioWatch Gen–3. On April 24, 2014, I convened an ARB and requested that the Science & Technology Directorate work with the BioWatch program office to improve our biodetection capability by exploring the development and maturation of an effective and affordable automated aerosol biodetection system.

CONCLUSION

DHS has worked diligently to improve its acquisition processes and these efforts have produced more effective governance and significant improvements to future and current acquisitions. The BioWatch Gen–3 program is an example of the successful application of the Department's improved acquisition oversight process because it ultimately led to the correct decision that the level of maturity of the technology was not sufficient at this date to justify proceeding. As the Department's Chief Acquisition Officer, I will continue to evaluate the risk of this and other programs, and will only provide authorization to proceed when pre-established criteria are met.

While there is still much work to do, the Department has made significant strides in improving acquisition and investment management for the Department's portfolio of major programs. I believe we are making progress in shifting the paradigm so investment decisions are more empirically driven and there is qualified technical expertise to support program managers at each phase of the life cycle.

Mrs. BROOKS. Thank you, Mr. Cummiskey.

The Chairman now recognizes Mr. Currie for 5 minutes. Thank you.

STATEMENT OF CHRIS CURRIE, ACTING DIRECTOR, HOMELAND SECURITY AND JUSTICE ISSUES, U.S. GOVERNMENT ACCOUNTABILITY OFFICE

Mr. CURRIE. Thank you, Chairman Brooks and Ranking Member Payne, other Members of the subcommittee. I appreciate the opportunity to be here today.

Today I would like to focus on the past, present, and the future of the BioWatch program. There are three areas I would like to discuss.

First are lessons learned from the Generation–3 acquisition. Second, are concerns our work has raised about DHS research and development efforts. Third are observations we have and questions that should be answered as the BioWatch program moves ahead.

Regarding the Gen–3 acquisition, lessons can definitely be learned. We reported that DHS pursued the Gen–3 technology without always following its acquisition policies. For example, we previously recommended that DHS conduct a robust analysis of program alternatives, the AOA, and cost estimate for Gen–3.

Prior program decisions were made without this information.

DHS listened. The more robust AOA they completed last year and updated cost estimate provided better information to make a cost-benefit decision about the program. DHS ultimately decided to cancel Gen–3 based on that information.

While opinions will differ on whether Gen–3 was a failure or not, what is clear is that DHS made the decision to cancel by following its acquisition processes.

This is encouraging progress because as this committee knows, and as you mentioned in your opening statement, Madam Chairwoman, failure to follow its acquisition policies is a major reason that DHS management is still on GAO's high-risk list.

My second point today pertains more specifically to the Science and Technology Directorate. Our body of work on DHS research and development, or R&D, raises management concerns that could impact S&T's efforts to develop future biodetection technologies.

More specifically, we reported in 2012 that DHS had no policies at the time for defining, overseeing, or coordinating R&D across the whole Department. As a result, R&D efforts were fragmented and overlapping, which could lead to unnecessary duplication.

Further, while S&T had agreements in place to transfer technologies to other DHS components, none of these at the time had resulted in a technology actually being transitioned to implementation. Also, some DHS component officials did not view coordination with S&T positively.

We made a number of recommendations to address these issues. DHS agreed, and they are making progress in addressing them. However, efforts are early and it is too soon to tell what impact these efforts are going to have.

The third area I would like to discuss are observations to consider as the BioWatch program moves ahead. For years, the focus has been on developing the Gen–3 system. Now that there is no Gen–3 to replace it, there are new questions about the performance and maintainability of the current system that need to be answered.

For example, DHS officials told us that some Gen–2 equipment is nearing the end of its useful life and will need to be replaced as early as next year. But it is not yet clear how the current system will be replaced or upgraded.

Also while Gen–2 has been used in the field for more than a decade now, information about its technical capabilities, including the limits of detection, is actually pretty limited.

For example, in 2011 the National Academy of Sciences reported that rapid initial deployment of BioWatch did not allow for sufficient testing and evaluation.

I would like to close with one last broader point today. This February, as you noted, your committee held a hearing on the overall bioterror threat. With the Gen–3 cancellation and Gen–2 system nearing the end of its life, DHS and its partners have an opportunity right now to assess the overall strategy for biosurveillance and how technology fits into it.

In July 2012, the White House issued the National Strategy for Biosurveillance. However, it didn't include a way to identify investment priorities among various biosurveillance efforts, such as how much do we invest in detection technologies?

These details were to be part of an implementation plan to follow, as you noted, the National strategy, but it has not been issued yet. We think these details will be very important to inform DHS decisions moving ahead.

This completes my prepared remarks. I would be pleased to answer any questions you have.

[The prepared statement of Mr. Currie follows:]

PREPARED STATEMENT OF CHRIS CURRIE

JUNE 10, 2014

GAO HIGHLIGHTS

Highlights of GAO–14–267T, a testimony before the Subcommittee on Emergency Preparedness, Response, and Communications, Committee on Homeland Security, House of Representatives.

Why GAO Did This Study

DHS's BioWatch program aims to detect the presence of biological agents considered to be at a high risk for weaponized attack in major U.S. cities. Initially, development of a next generation technology (Gen–3) was led by DHS S&T, with the goal of improving upon currently-deployed technology (Gen–2). Gen–3 would have potentially enabled collection and analysis of air samples in less than 6 hours, unlike Gen–2 which can take up to 36 hours to detect and confirm the presence of biological pathogens. Since fiscal year 2007, OHA has been responsible for overseeing the acquisition of this technology. GAO has published a series of reports on biosurveillance efforts, including a report on DHS's Gen–3 acquisition.

In April 2014, DHS canceled the acquisition of Gen–3 and plans to move development efforts of an affordable automated aerosol biodetection capability, or other enhancements to the BioWatch system to DHS S&T. This statement addresses: (1) Observations from GAO's prior work on the acquisition processes for Gen–3, and the current status of the program; (2) observations from GAO's prior work related to

DHS S&T and the impact it could have on the BioWatch program; and (3) future considerations for the currently deployed Gen–2 system.

This testimony is based on previous GAO reports issued from 2010 through 2014 related to biosurveillance and research and development, and selected updates obtained from January to June 2014. For these updates, GAO reviewed studies and documents and interviewed officials from DHS and the National labs, which have performed studies for DHS.

BIOSURVEILLANCE.—OBSERVATIONS ON THE CANCELLATION OF BIOWATCH GEN–3 AND FUTURE CONSIDERATIONS FOR THE PROGRAM

What GAO Found

In September 2012, GAO reported that the Department of Homeland Security (DHS) approved the Office of Health Affairs (OHA) acquisition of a next generation biosurveillance technology (Gen–3) in October 2009 without fully following its acquisition processes. For example, the analysis of alternatives (AoA) prepared for the Gen–3 acquisition did not fully explore costs or consider benefits and risk information in accordance with DHS's Acquisition Life-cycle Framework. To help ensure DHS based its acquisition decisions on reliable performance, cost, and schedule information, GAO recommended that before continuing the Gen–3 acquisition, DHS reevaluate the mission need and alternatives. DHS concurred with the recommendation and in 2012 decided to reassess mission needs and conduct a more robust AoA. Following the issuance of the AoA in December 2013, DHS decided in April 2014 to cancel Gen–3 acquisition and move the technology development back to the Science and Technology Directorate (S&T). According to DHS's acquisition decisions memorandum, the AoA did not confirm an overwhelming benefit to justify the cost of a full technology switch to Gen–3. Moreover, DHS officials said the decision to cancel the Gen–3 acquisition was a cost-effectiveness measure, because the system was going to be too costly to develop and maintain in its current form.

GAO's prior work on DHS research and development (R&D) highlights challenges DHS may face in shifting efforts back to S&T and acquiring another biodetection technology. In September 2012, GAO reported that while S&T had dozens of technology transition agreements with DHS components, none of these had yet resulted in a technology developed by S&T being used by a component. At the same time, other DHS component officials GAO interviewed did not view S&T's coordination practices positively. GAO recommended that DHS develop and implement policies and guidance for defining and overseeing R&D at the Department that includes a well-understood definition of R&D that provides reasonable assurance that reliable accounting and reporting of R&D resources and activities for internal and external use are achieved. S&T agreed with GAO's recommendations and efforts to address them are on-going. Addressing these coordination challenges could help to ensure that S&T's technology development efforts meet the operational needs of OHA.

Cancellation of the Gen–3 acquisition also raises potential challenges that the currently deployed Gen–2 system could face going forward. According to DHS officials, DHS will continue to rely on its Gen–2 system as an early indicator of an aerosolized biological attack. However, in 2011, National Academy of Sciences raised questions about the effectiveness of the currently deployed Gen–2 system. While Gen–2 has been used in the field for over a decade, the National Academy of Sciences reported that information about the technical capabilities of the system, including the limits of detection, is limited. In April 2014, DHS officials also indicated that they will soon need to replace laboratory equipment of the currently-deployed Gen–2 system and readjust life-cycle costs since there will be no Gen–3 technology to replace it.

Chairman Brooks, Ranking Member Payne, and Members of the subcommittee: I am pleased to be here today to discuss our observations on the Department of Homeland Security's (DHS) BioWatch program, with particular focus on the cancellation of BioWatch Generation–3 (Gen–3) and future considerations for the program. In recent years, there has been an increasing awareness of the potential for biological agents to be used as weapons of mass destruction. Experts and practitioners, reacting to an increasing awareness of the speed and intensity with which a biological weapon of mass destruction could affect the Nation, have sought to augment traditional surveillance activities with biosurveillance programs and systems.[1]

---

[1] Traditional disease surveillance activities involve trained professionals engaged in monitoring, investigating, confirming, and reporting in an effort to further various missions including, but not limited to, detecting signs of pathogens in humans, animals, plants, food, and the environment. The National Strategy for Biosurveillance defines "biosurveillance" as the process of gathering, integrating, interpreting, and communicating essential information related to all-

DHS's BioWatch program is an example of such an effort. BioWatch aims to reduce the time required to recognize and characterize potentially catastrophic aerosolized attacks by detecting the presence of five biological agents—considered to be at a high risk for weaponized attack—in the air.

DHS's Office of Health Affairs (OHA) oversees the currently-deployed BioWatch technology—Generation–2 (Gen–2)—which can take 12 to 36 hours to confirm the presence of pathogens. Until recently, DHS had been pursuing a next-generation technology (Gen–3) with the goal of improving upon existing technology by enabling autonomous collection and analysis of air samples using the same laboratory science that is carried out in manual processes to operate the current system (e.g., lab-in-a-box). The new technology would have reduced detection time, potentially generating a result in under 6 hours, and eliminated certain labor costs.

This statement includes observations from our prior work: (1) On DHS's acquisition processes for Gen–3, and the current status of the program; (2) related to DHS's Science and Technology Directorate (S&T) and the impact it could have on the BioWatch program; and (3) future considerations for the currently-deployed Gen–2 system.

This testimony is based on our previous reports issued from 2010 through 2014 related to biosurveillance, research and development, and acquisitions.[2] For this work, we reviewed DHS's acquisition guidance, including Acquisition Management Directive 102–01. Additionally, we reviewed acquisition documentation and interviewed agency officials from the BioWatch program and other DHS offices with development, policy, and acquisition responsibilities. We then compared the information developed from our documentation review and interviews against the guidance. We also interviewed S&T leadership, technical division directors, and DHS component officials to discuss S&T and DHS's research and development (R&D) coordination processes. More detailed information on our scope and methodology appears in the published reports. This statement is also based in part on selected updates we conducted in June 2013 and July 2013 related to DHS's R&D efforts and its oversight of R&D efforts across the Department and on selected updates related to the BioWatch program conducted from January to June 2014.[3] For updates on the BioWatch program, we analyzed studies and documents and interviewed knowledgeable officials at DHS and the National laboratories, which have performed testing and studies for DHS.

We conducted the work upon which this statement is based and the selected updates in accordance with generally accepted Government auditing standards. Those standards require that we plan and perform the audit to obtain sufficient, appropriate evidence to provide a reasonable basis for our findings and conclusions based on our audit objectives. We believe that the evidence obtained provides a reasonable basis for our findings and conclusions based on our audit objectives. Additional details on our scope and methodology can be found in the individual products cited throughout this statement.

---

hazards threats or disease activity affecting human, animal, or plant health to achieve early detection and warning, contribute to overall situational awareness of the health aspects of an incident, and enable better decision making at all levels.

[2] GAO, *Biosurveillance: Efforts to Develop a National Biosurveillance Capability Need a National Strategy and a Designated Leader*, GAO–10–645 (Washington, DC: June 30, 2010). GAO, *Department of Homeland Security: Oversight and Coordination of Research and Development Should Be Strengthened*, GAO–12–837 (Washington, DC: Sept. 12, 2012). GAO, *Biosurveillance: Observations on BioWatch Generation–3 and Other Federal Efforts*. GAO–12–994T (Washington, DC, Sept. 2012). GAO–13–279SP. GAO, *Biosurveillance: DHS Should Reevaluate Mission Need and Alternatives before Proceeding with BioWatch Generation–3 Acquisition*, GAO–12–810 (Washington, DC: Sept. 10, 2012). GAO, *Department of Homeland Security: Opportunities Exist to Strengthen Efficiency and Effectiveness, Achieve Cost Savings, and Improve Management Functions*, GAO–13–547T (Washington, DC: April 26, 2013). GAO, *Department of Homeland Security: Oversight and Coordination of Research and Development Efforts Could Be Strengthened*, GAO–13–766T (Washington, DC, July 17, 2013). GAO, *Canceled DOD Programs: DOD Needs to Better Use Available Guidance and Manage Reusable Assets*, GAO–14–77 (Washington, DC: Mar. 27, 2014). GAO, *Homeland Security: Acquisitions: DHS Could Better Manage Its Portfolio To Address Funding Gaps and Improve Communications With Congress*, GAO–14–332, (Washington, DC, April 2014).

[3] GAO–13–766T.

BACKGROUND

DHS Acquisitions and the Cancellation of Gen–3

We have highlighted DHS acquisition management issues in our high-risk list since 2005.[4] Over the past several years, our work has identified significant shortcomings in the Department's ability to manage an expanding portfolio of major acquisitions.[5] We have also reported that while DHS acquisition policy reflects many key program management practices intended to mitigate the risks of cost growth and schedule slips, the Department did not implement the policy consistently.[6] In 2011, expressing concerns about whether DHS had undertaken a rigorous effort to help guide its Gen–3 decision making, Members of Congress asked us to examine issues related to the Gen–3 acquisition. We released a report that evaluated the acquisition decision-making process for Gen–3 in September 2012.[7] As discussed later in the statement, we recommended that before continuing the Gen–3 acquisition, DHS should carry out key acquisition steps, including reevaluating the mission need and systematically analyzing alternatives based on cost-benefit and risk information.[8]

On April 24, 2014, DHS issued an Acquisition Decision Memo (ADM) announcing the cancellation of the acquisition of Gen–3.[9] The ADM also announced that S&T will explore development and maturation of an effective and affordable automated aerosol biodetection capability, or other operational enhancements, that meet the operational requirements of the BioWatch system.[10] DHS's S&T conducts research, development, testing, and evaluation of new technologies that are intended to strengthen the United States' ability to prevent and respond to nuclear, biological, explosive, and other types of attacks within the United States. S&T has six technical divisions responsible for managing S&T's research R&D portfolio and coordinating with other DHS components to identify R&D priorities and needs.[11] Most of S&T's R&D portfolio consists of applied research and development projects for its DHS customers.

BioWatch in Action

The BioWatch program collaborates with 30 BioWatch jurisdictions throughout the Nation to operate approximately 600 Gen–2 collectors. These detectors rely on a vacuum-based collection system that draws air samples through a filter. These filters must be manually collected and transported to State and local public health laboratories for analysis using a process called Polymerase Chain Reaction (PCR). During this process, the sample is evaluated for the presence of genetic material from five different biological agents. If genetic material is detected, a BioWatch Ac-

[4] GAO, *High-Risk Series: An Update,* GAO–05–207 (Washington, DC: January 2005).

[5] For examples, see GAO, *Homeland Security: DHS Requires More Disciplined Investment Management to Help Meet Mission Needs,* GAO–12–833 (Washington, DC: Sept. 18, 2012); *Department of Homeland Security: Assessments of Selected Complex Acquisitions,* GAO–10–588SP (Washington, DC: June 30, 2010); and *Department of Homeland Security: Billions Invested in Major Programs Lack Appropriate Oversight,* GAO–09–29 (Washington, DC: Nov. 18, 2008).

[6] GAO, *Department of Homeland Security: Progress Made; Significant Work Remains in Addressing High-Risk Areas,* GAO–14–532T (Washington, DC: May 7, 2014). The reference to DHS acquisition policy, for purposes of this testimony, consists of Management Directive (ADM) 102–01, and an associated guidebook. The overall policy and structure for acquisition management outlined in DHS's AMD 102–01 includes the Department's Acquisition Life-cycle Framework—a template for planning and executing acquisitions. DHS's Acquisition Life-cycle Framework includes four acquisition phases through which DHS determines whether it is sensible to proceed with a proposed acquisition: (1) Identify a capability need; (2) analyze and select the optimal solution to meet that need; (3) obtain the solution; and (4) produce, deploy, and support the solution.

[7] GAO–12–810.

[8] The Gen–3 acquisition was in the early stages of Phase 3 (obtain the solution) when the acquisition was placed on hold.

[9] An Acquisition Decision Memo (ADM) is the official record of the Acquisition Decision Event and describes the decisions made and any action items to be satisfied as conditions of the decision made by the Acquisition Review Board.

[10] DHS began to develop autonomous detection technology in 2003. Initially, development of technologies to support autonomous detection was led by DHS's S&T, which partnered with industry. Since fiscal year 2007, DHS's OHA has been responsible for overseeing the acquisition of this technology.

[11] These divisions are the Borders and Maritime Division, Chemical/Biological Defense Division, Cyber Security Division, Explosives Division, Human Factors/Behavioral Sciences Division, and the Infrastructure Protection and Disaster Management Division. In addition, S&T's First Responder Group (FRG) identifies, validates, and facilitates the fulfillment of first responder requirements through the use of existing and emerging technologies, knowledge products, and the development of technical standards, according to S&T FRG officials.

tionable Result (BAR) is declared. Figure 1 shows the process that local BioWatch jurisdictions are to follow when deciding how to respond to a BAR.[12]

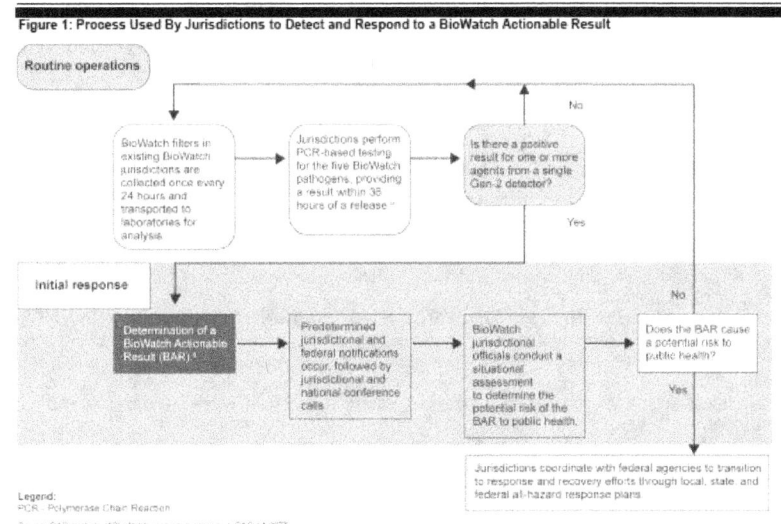

Figure 1: Process Used By Jurisdictions to Detect and Respond to a BioWatch Actionable Result

OUR PRIOR WORK ON THE GEN–3 ACQUISITION IDENTIFIED CHALLENGES AND DHS HAS SINCE CANCELED THE PROGRAM

Our prior findings and recommendations related to the Gen–3 acquisition provide DHS with lessons learned for future decision making. In September 2012, we found that DHS approved the Gen–3 acquisition in October 2009 without fully developing critical knowledge that would help ensure sound investment decision making, pursuit of optimal solutions, and reliable performance, cost, and schedule information. Specifically, we found that DHS did not engage the initial phase of its Acquisition Life-cycle Framework, which is designed to help ensure that the mission need driving the acquisition warrants investment of limited resources.[13] BioWatch officials stated that they were aware that the Mission Needs Statement prepared in October 2009 did not reflect a systematic effort to justify a capability need, but stated that the Department directed them to proceed because there was already Departmental consensus around the solution. Accordingly, we concluded that the utility of the Mission Needs Statement as a foundation for subsequent acquisition efforts was limited.

Additionally, in September 2012, we found that DHS did not use the processes established by its Acquisition Life-cycle Framework to systematically ensure that it was pursuing the optimal solution—based on cost, benefit, and risk—to mitigate the

---

[12] The BioWatch program defines a BAR as one or more Polymerase Chain Reaction (PCR)-verified positive results from a single BioWatch collector. A positive result requires multiple strands of the PCR-amplified DNA to match an algorithm that has been designed to indicate the presence of genetic material from one or more of the agents in question.

[13] According to DHS officials, the Gen–3 acquisition was on-going when Acquisition Management Directive 102–01 was issued. The officials said that many DHS programs that were on-going in 2009 faced similar challenges. Nevertheless, DHS Management Directive 1400, which preceded Acquisition Management Directive 102–01, was similarly designed to, among other things, ensure that investments directly support and further DHS's missions. Like Acquisition Management Directive 102–01, Management Directive 1400 describes a phased life-cycle investment construct in which the first step is defining the mission need in a Mission Needs Statement. As with the Mission Need Statement called for in Acquisition Management Directive 102–01, the statement in Management Directive 1400 was to be a high-level description of a capability gap rather than a specific solution.

capability gap identified in the Mission Needs Statement. The DHS Acquisition Life-cycle Framework calls for the program office to develop an analysis of alternatives (AoA) that systematically identifies possible alternative solutions that could satisfy the identified need, considers cost-benefit and risk information for each alternative, and finally selects the best option from among the alternatives. However, we found that the AoA prepared for the Gen–3 acquisition did not reflect a systematic deci-sion-making process. For example, in addition to—or perhaps reflecting—its origin in a predetermined solution from the Mission Needs Statement, the AoA did not fully explore costs or consider benefits and risk information as part of the analysis. Instead, the AoA focused on just one cost metric that justified the decision to pursue autonomous detection—cost per detection cycle—to the exclusion of other cost and benefit considerations that might have further informed decision makers.[14] Addi-tionally, we found that the AoA examined only two alternatives, though the guid-ance calls for at least three. The first alternative was the currently deployed Gen-2 technology with a modified operational model (which by definition was unable to meet the established goals). The second alternative was the complete replacement of the deployed Gen–2 program with an autonomous detection technology and ex-panded deployment.

As we reported in September 2012, BioWatch program officials acknowledged that other options—including but not limited to deploying some combination of both tech-nologies (the currently-deployed system and an autonomous detection system), based on risk and logistical considerations—may be more cost-effective. As with the Mis-sion Needs Statement, program officials told us that they were advised that a com-prehensive AoA would not be necessary because there was already Departmental consensus that autonomous detection was the optimal solution. Because the Gen–3 AoA did not: Evaluate a complete solution set; consider complete information on cost and benefits; and include a cost-benefit analysis, we concluded that it did not provide information on which to base trade-off decisions.

To help ensure DHS based its acquisition decisions on reliable performance, cost, and schedule information developed in accordance with guidance and good practices, in our September 2012 report, we recommended that before continuing the Gen–3 acquisition, DHS reevaluate the mission need and possible alternatives based on cost-benefit and risk information. DHS concurred with the recommendation and in 2012, DHS directed the BioWatch program to complete an updated AoA.[15]

DHS contracted with the Institute for Defense Analyses (IDA) to conduct the up-dated AoA, which they issued in December 2013. In January 2014, as part of rec-ommendation follow-up, we reviewed the completed analysis. IDA cited the *DHS Ac-quisition Management Instruction/Guidebook* and its appendix on conducting an AoA as the criteria for their study. The management directive lays out a sample framework that details the specific steps to take in evaluating acquisition alter-natives, which the contractor used for completing its study. On the basis of our re-view, we concluded that the IDA-conducted AoA followed the DHS guidance and re-sulted in a more robust exploration of alternatives than the previous effort. The AoA was not intended to identify a specific solution to address DHS's requirements for earlier warning and detection capabilities. According to IDA, the AoA does not claim to select a solution, but rather to present alternatives and the information required to select an alternative based on cost and effectiveness trade-offs.

On April 24, 2014, the DHS Acquisition Review Board reviewed the BioWatch Gen–3 acquisition with OHA and issued an ADM announcing the cancellation of the acquisition of Gen–3. According to the DHS ADM, the AoA "did not confirm an over-whelming benefit to justify the cost of a full technology switch" to Gen–3. The ADM also announced that S&T will explore development and maturation of an effective and affordable automated aerosol biodetection capability, or other operational en-hancements, that meet the operational requirements of the BioWatch system.

In April 2014, BioWatch Program officials said multiple factors influenced the de-cision to end the Gen–3 acquisition, including budget considerations, considerations regarding the readiness level of the technology, and the cost to field and maintain the technology. BioWatch Program officials said that the Homeland Security Studies and Analysis Institute's and our recommendations to complete a robust AoA, which resulted in not identifying a clear path forward for a single technology type for the Gen–3 acquisition, was also a contributing factor. According to BioWatch Program

---

[14] Cost per detection cycle is the cost each time an autonomous detector tests the air for patho-gens or the cost each time a Gen–2 filter is manually collected and tested in a laboratory.

[15] According to DHS's Acquisition Life-cycle Framework, an Analysis of Alternatives system-atically identifies possible alternative solutions that could satisfy the identified need, considers cost-benefit and risk information for each alternative, and finally selects the best option from among the alternatives.

officials, DHS has not ruled out the possibility of pursuing autonomous detection for the BioWatch program, but officials said the technology would have to cost less to develop and maintain than was estimated for the Gen–3 system.

Earlier this year, we reported that when programs have been canceled, cost, schedule, and performance problems have often been cited as reasons for this decision, and cancellation can be perceived as failure.[16] However, in some circumstances, program cancellation may be the best choice. In an April 2014 interview, BioWatch Program officials said the Gen–3 acquisitions process yielded many benefits, despite its cancellation. BioWatch Program officials said the program office has learned and gained much from this experience, including engaging State and local stakeholders to help ensure confidence in the system and BioWatch program; finding better ways to test technologies and refine the Testing and Evaluation guidance; and developing robust acquisition documentation for the Department. BioWatch program officials said the decision to cancel the Gen–3 acquisition was a cost-effectiveness measure, because the system was going to be too costly to develop and maintain in its current form. We reported in 2012 that while the DHS June 2011 life-cycle cost estimate reported $104 million in actual and estimated costs from fiscal year 2008 through fiscal year 2011, it also indicated that Gen–3 was expected to cost $5.8 billion (80 percent confidence) from fiscal year 2012 through June 2028. However, the original life-cycle cost estimate for the 2009 decision—a point estimate unadjusted for risk—was $2.1 billion.[17]

DHS R&D EFFORTS ALSO FACE CHALLENGES THAT COULD IMPACT THE BIOWATCH PROGRAM

DHS has taken positive steps as we recommended to complete a robust assessment of the available biodetection technology alternatives and has taken into consideration the cost and readiness level of the current technology. However, our prior work reviewing DHS research and development efforts highlights challenges DHS may face in transitioning the future biodetection development efforts S&T is now charged with exploring back to the program office, OHA. For example, S&T works with DHS components to ensure that it meets their R&D needs by signing technology transition agreements (TTA) to ensure that components use the technologies S&T develops. However, we previously reported in September 2012 that while S&T had 42 TTAs with DHS components, none of these TTAs has yet resulted in a technology being transitioned from S&T to a component.[18] In that review we also found that other DHS component officials we interviewed did not view S&T's coordination practices positively. Specifically, we interviewed officials in six components to discuss the extent to which they coordinated with S&T on R&D activities. Officials in four components stated that S&T did not have an established process that detailed how S&T would work with its customers or for coordinating all activities at DHS. For example, officials in one component stated that S&T has conducted R&D that it thought would address the component's operational need but, when work was completed, the R&D project did not fit into the operational environment to meet the component's needs.

We also reported in 2012 that OHA, which oversees operation of the BioWatch program, and S&T already had a history of working together on advancing the technology used by the BioWatch program.[19] However, differences of opinion on key performance measures had created a challenge for these two offices related to future biodetection technologies. For example, during our 2012 review of the Gen–3 acquisition, officials from OHA said both OHA and S&T commissioned the Sandia National Laboratory to conduct similar studies on the performance characteristics of the Gen–3 autonomous detection system, but the two offices requested the use of different performance metrics to evaluate Gen–3's detection capability. OHA officials said they supported using the fraction of the population covered as the metric because it is directly related to public health outcomes, while S&T preferred to use the probability of detection. While we recognize there are advantages and disadvantages for choosing different performance metrics, technology transition of the R&D

---

[16] GAO–14–77.

[17] We reported in 2012 that this point estimate was not completed in accordance with the GAO Cost Estimating Guide, which DHS uses for cost estimating to help ensure the reliability of its cost estimates. According to the Guide, a point estimate, by itself, provides no information about the underlying uncertainty other than that it is the value chosen as most likely. A confidence interval, in contrast, provides a range of possible costs, based on a specified probability level. See, GAO, *Cost Estimating and Assessment Guide,* GAO–09–3SP (Washington, DC: Mar. 2, 2009).

[18] GAO–12–837.

[19] GAO–12–810.

project developed by S&T could prove challenging in the future if fundamental differences like this are not resolved early to help ensure the technology meets the operational needs of the program office.

In our September 2012 report, we concluded that DHS and S&T could be in a better position to coordinate the Department's R&D efforts by implementing a specific policy outlining R&D roles, responsibilities, and processes for coordinating R&D. As a result, we recommended that DHS develop and implement policies and guidance for defining and overseeing R&D at the Department-level that includes a well-understood definition of R&D that provides reasonable assurance that reliable accounting and reporting of R&D resources and activities for internal and external use are achieved. DHS agreed with our recommendation, and in April 2014, updated its guidance to include a definition of R&D, but efforts to develop a specific policy outlining R&D roles and responsibilities and a process for coordinating R&D with other offices remain on-going and have not yet been completed.[20]

FUTURE CONSIDERATIONS FOR THE CURRENTLY-DEPLOYED GEN–2 SYSTEM

With the cancellation of the Gen–3 acquisition, DHS will continue to rely on its currently deployed Gen–2 system as an early indicator of an aerosolized biological attack. Cancellation of the Gen–3 system also raises questions that need to be answered about the future maintenance of the Gen–2 system, since it will no longer be replaced, as planned. According to program officials that we recently contacted, DHS is considering multiple options to upgrade the current technology to improve detection capabilities in the wake of the Gen–3 acquisition cancellation. In April 2014, program officials described some of the options they are considering to upgrade the currently deployed system, including:

- The addition of a trigger to the current system to enhance performance indoors. These are generally systems that provide very fast but nonspecific warnings of a potential agent release, because they do not identify the type of biological material detected. However, DHS is exploring how to use a trigger to indicate when an air sample should be collected and taken to the laboratory for analysis.
- Use of a wet or liquid filter system rather than the current dry filter system. Collecting samples directly into a liquid could also increase the odds that any microorganisms would remain alive for subsequent testing.
- Increased frequency of manual filter collection and testing, which would likely increase costs.
- Other options for hand-held or portable detection devices.

While OHA officials determine the next steps with S&T for the BioWatch program to try and address the capability gap that Gen–3 intended to fill, there are other considerations for the currently-deployed system, such as maintainability of the current technology and equipment and the costs associated with any upgrades to extend the life of the existing system. For example, BioWatch program officials indicated they will need to replace the laboratory equipment for the currently-deployed system, as early as 2015, and readjust life-cycle costs.[21]

Further, while Gen–2 has been used in the field for over a decade, information about the technical capabilities for the Gen–2 system, including the limits of detection, is limited. In 2011, the National Academy of Sciences stated that the rapid initial deployment of BioWatch did not allow for sufficient testing, validation, and evaluation of the system and its components.[22] The National Academies evaluation of BioWatch noted there is considerable uncertainty about the likelihood and magnitude of a biological attack, and how the risk of a release of an aerosolized pathogen compares with risks from other potential forms of terrorism or from natural diseases. Further, the report also stated that to achieve its health protection goals, the BioWatch system should be better linked to a broader and more effective National biosurveillance framework that will help provide State and local public health authorities, in collaboration with the health care system, with the information they need to determine the appropriate response to a possible or confirmed attack or disease outbreak.

Our prior work has also highlighted the uncertainty about the incremental benefit of this kind of environmental monitoring as a risk mitigation activity because of its relatively limited scope and the challenges agencies face in making these investment

---

[20] *The DHS Delegation to the Under Secretary for Science and Technology,* DHS Delegation Number: 10001, Revision Number: 01, Annex A includes the definition for research and development.

[21] The Consolidated Appropriations Act, 2014, appropriated the Office of Health Affairs $85 million for BioWatch operations. Pub. L. No. 113–76, 128 Stat. 5, 260.

[22] See Institute of Medicine and National Research Council, *BioWatch and Public Health Surveillance,* 2011.

decisions. In our June 2010 report on Federal biosurveillance efforts, we recommended the Homeland Security Council direct the National Security Staff to identify a focal point to lead the development of a National biosurveillance strategy. We made this recommendation because we recognized the difficulty that decision makers and program managers in individual Federal agencies face prioritizing resources to help ensure a coherent effort across a vast and dispersed interagency, intergovernmental, and intersectoral network. Therefore, we called for a strategy that would, among other things: (1) Define the scope and purpose of a National capability; (2) provide goals, objectives and activities, priorities, milestones, and performance measures; and (3) assess the costs and benefits and identify resource and investment needs, including investment priorities.[23] In July 2012, the White House released the National Strategy for Biosurveillance to describe the U.S. Government's approach to strengthening biosurveillance, but it does not fully meet the intent of our prior recommendations, because it does not yet offer a mechanism to identify resource and investment needs, including investment priorities among various biosurveillance efforts. We remain hopeful that the forthcoming strategic implementation plan which was supposed to be issued in October 2012 and promised to include specific actions and activity scope, designated roles and responsibilities, and a mechanism for evaluating progress will help to address the on-going need for mechanisms that will help prioritize resource allocation. However, as of March 14, 2014 the implementation plan had not been released.

Chairman Brooks, Ranking Member Payne, and Members of the subcommittee, this concludes my prepared statement. I would be happy to respond to any questions you may have.

Mrs. BROOKS. Thank you, Mr. Currie.

The Chairwoman now recognizes Dr. Disraelly for 5 minutes.

STATEMENT OF DEENA S. DISRAELLY, RESEARCH STAFF, STRATEGY, FORCES, AND RESOURCES DIVISION, INSTITUTE FOR DEFENSE ANALYSES

Ms. DISRAELLY. Thank you, Chairman Brooks, Ranking Member Payne, and distinguished Members of the subcommittee for inviting me to speak with you today. My name is Dr. Deena Disraelly and I am a research staff member at the Institute for Defense Analyses and the team leader on the BioWatch Analysis of Alternatives. I am honored to be here today to discuss our work with you.

The Institute for Defense Analyses is a Federally-funded research and development center assisting the Department of Defense and other Federal agencies in addressing important National security issues, particularly those requiring scientific and technical expertise.

We were tasked by the BioWatch program office within the Department of Homeland Security to conduct an Analysis of Alternatives subsequent to the Government Accountability Office report on biosurveillance and the BioWatch Gen–3 acquisition.

Our study is documented in the BioWatch Analysis of Alternatives, which is summarized very briefly in the written testimony we submitted.

Based on the Department's guidance, an Analysis of Alternatives provides the systematic, analytic, and decision-making process to facilitate identification of an optimal solution for an identified capability gap.

In this case, the capability gap was established in Homeland Security Presidential Directive–10, which called for early warning, detection, or recognition of biological weapons attacks to permit a timely response to mitigate their consequences.

---

[23] GAO–10–645.

The intent of the Analysis of Alternatives was to identify material and non-material biological surveillance capabilities, with the potential to reduce casualties resulting from the release of an aerosolized pathogen, and to conduct our study in accordance with the Department's guidance documents on established metrics and methodologies.

It was not within the scope of our study to provide a recommendation about the disposition of the BioWatch Gen–3 system.

Following a review of approximately 500 biological surveillance capabilities, we identified four candidate alternatives, each with an anticipated operational capability to perform the BioWatch mission and concepts of operation to detect an aerosolized biological event.

Autonomous identification systems are labs in a box that collect and test environmental samples on site. Environmental collection systems collect environmental samples that are then picked up and transported to an off-site laboratory for analysis.

The Sentinel population alternative involves police officers carrying lightweight portable collectors for subsequent laboratory sample analysis.

Clinical diagnosis and diagnostics are a combination of technologies and activities used to identify disease in symptomatic individuals and notify the appropriate public health authorities.

The Analysis of Alternatives provides the Government decision-makers a framework for thinking about the trade-offs among the alternatives examined. Our findings can be summarized as follows.

Clinical diagnosis and diagnostics is the least expensive alternative, and was assumed to have a probability of detection of 100 percent because every disease is eventually diagnosed. However, diagnosis takes time and detection of an event requires some number of diagnosed cases. Therefore this alternative also had the highest number of casualties.

The Sentinel population alternative had a high probability of detection, and those detections happened relatively quickly, resulting in lower numbers of casualties. That probability of detection is achieved with a large number of roving detectors, meaning a large number of samples processed several times a day.

The result is a life-cycle cost estimate four times that of environmental collection and autonomous identification.

Environmental collection is currently deployed, as has been noted, and is less expensive than autonomous identification. However, it also takes longer to identify agents, which may lead to an increase in casualties for detected attacks.

Autonomous identification has a slightly higher life-cycle cost estimate than environmental collection. Additionally, while it achieves the fastest detections, when it detects, it only detects on average approximately half the number of attacks detected by environmental collection, resulting in increased numbers of casualties due to large numbers of missed attacks.

HSPD–10 is still in effect and, as such, the imperative remains for an early warning and detection system to identify biological events and trigger a response to mitigate their consequences. Our Analysis of Alternatives provided objective, analytical information to support DHS's decision-making with regard to that directive.

This concludes my opening remarks. Thank you.

[The prepared statement of Ms. Disraelly follows:]

PREPARED STATEMENT OF DEENA S. DISRAELLY

JUNE 2014

A. INTRODUCTION

Good morning Chairman Brooks, Ranking Member Payne, and distinguished Members of the House Subcommittee on Emergency Preparedness, Response, and Communication. My name is Dr. Deena Disraelly. I am a research staff member at the Institute for Defense Analyses (IDA) and the project lead for the BioWatch Analysis of Alternatives (AoA). I am honored to appear before you today to discuss this study and its results.

In October 2012, the BioWatch Program Office asked IDA, a Federally-Funded Research and Development Center (FFRDC) assisting the Department of Defense and other Federal agencies in addressing issues of National security, to conduct an AoA of capabilities to meet the biosurveillance mission. According to U.S. Department of Homeland Security (DHS) guidance, an AoA provides "a systematic analytic and decision-making process to identify and document an optimal solution for an identified mission capability gap."[1] The BioWatch AoA addresses a capability gap identified in Homeland Security Presidential Directive (HSPD)–10 *Biodefense for the 21st Century,* namely the requirement for an "early warning, detection, or recognition of biological weapons attacks to permit a timely response to mitigate their consequences."[2] This AoA identified material (technology) and non-material (activity) biological surveillance capabilities—comprised of one or more technologies or related activities—with the potential to reduce mortality and morbidity from an aerosolized release of a pathogen. Specifically, the AoA focused on four candidate alternatives that will be defined later in this presentation.

While the objective of this study was to identify and compare capabilities, IDA was not asked to provide DHS with any recommendations about the disposition of the BioWatch Generation–3 (Gen–3) system.

The IDA team's *BioWatch Analysis of Alternatives*[3] was delivered to the BioWatch Program Office in December 2013. What follows is a brief discussion of the AoA objectives, methodology, and findings extracted from the more detailed discussion in that paper.

B. ANALYSIS OF ALTERNATIVES (AOA) BACKGROUND AND OBJECTIVES

In accordance with HSPD–10, the DHS BioWatch Program is intended to provide "a Nation-wide biosurveillance capability to monitor for select aerosolized biothreat agents in highly populated areas . . . and is a partnership between Federal, State, and local governments for the purpose of ensuring the protection of the Nation's population against biological threats."[4] The objective of the BioWatch collectors is to monitor the air continuously for agents of concern and provide regular analyses of the results. The goal is to field a system that is operational 24 hours per day, 365 days per year and able to signal an attack early enough to promote quick response.[5]

The BioWatch Program was created in 2003 "to provide early warning, detection, or recognition of biological attack."[6] The first environmental collectors (Generation–1) were deployed in March of 2003, with deployment eventually reaching 20 major metropolitan areas. The program began a second deployment (Generation–2) immediately in the wake of the previous deployment, adding ten jurisdictions and "indoor monitoring capabilities in three high-threat jurisdictions and provided additional capacity for events of national significance, such as major sporting events and political

---

[1] U.S. Department of Homeland Security (DHS), *Acquisition Management Instruction/Guidebook,* DHS Instruction Manual 102–01–001, Appendix G (Washington, DC: DHS, 2011), G–3.

[2] President George W. Bush, *Biodefense for the 21st Century* (hereafter: HSPD–10), Homeland Security Presidential Directive HSPD–10 (Washington, DC: The White House, 2004).

[3] Deena Disraelly et al., *BioWatch Analysis of Alternatives,* Institute for Defense Analyses (IDA), Paper P–5083 (Alexandria, VA: IDA, 2013).

[4] DHS, Office of Health Affairs (DHS/OHA), *Gen–3 [Generation–3] Autonomous Detection System, Operational Requirements Document (ORD) v 2.2* (hereafter: *Gen–3 ORD*) (Washington, DC: DHS, 2012), ES–1, For Official Use Only (FOUO).

[5] DHS/OHA, *Gen–3 ORD,* FOUO; Bush, *HSPD–10.*

[6] U.S. Government Accountability Office (GAO), *BioSurveillance: DHS Should Reevaluate Mission Need and Alternatives before Proceeding with BioWatch Generation–3 Acquisition* (hereafter: BioSurveillance—Reevaluate Mission Need), GAO–12–810 (Washington, DC: GAO, 2012), 9.

conventions."[7] Generation–1 and Generation–2 collectors are predominantly located in outdoor environments and the overall system, as currently implemented, relies on both the collectors and teams of field and laboratory personnel. The 2009 DHS Appropriations Act established the appropriations for an improved biodetection capability.

In 2010, DHS published its first *Acquisition Directive* (DHS Directive 102–01),[8] which requires DHS components pursuing acquisition programs to perform an AoA or Alternatives Analysis[9] during procurement. Two years later, the Homeland Security Studies and Analysis Institute published the *BioWatch Gen–3 Program Acquisition Assessment.* Soon after, the U.S. Government Accountability Office (GAO) published GAO–12–810, *BioSurveillance: DHS Should Reevaluate Mission Need and Alternatives Before Proceeding with BioWatch Gen–3 Acquisition.* Both reports recommended that the BioWatch Program Office perform an AoA for the BioWatch Program. Subsequently, the BioWatch Program Office asked IDA to conduct an AoA of biosurveillance capabilities in accordance with applicable DHS guidance.

C. AOA PROJECT METHODOLOGY

1. Methodology Overview

The first step in the AoA process was to consult relevant studies and literature on biosurveillance and conduct a market survey of all biosurveillance capabilities and their component technologies/activities (hereafter referred to simply as capabilities). During the course of the market survey, the IDA team identified approximately 500 biosurveillance capabilities that are either readily deployable or in development. Constraints were defined then used to identify selected candidate alternatives that could fulfill the BioWatch mission need and requirements.[10] Specifically, the selected candidate alternatives met the following constraints:

1. Include technologies and activities at, or equivalent to, technology readiness level (TRL) 6.[11]

2. Be available to deploy within 2 to 3 years and be fully fieldable within 2 to 5 years of the completion of the AoA.[12]

3. Be able to detect an aerosolized biological attack for, at least, the same five threshold biological agents as required for Gen–3.[13]

4. Are anticipated to be fully fieldable and sustainable within the budget already allocated for BioWatch over the next 5 years (the budget figure is in fiscal year 2013 dollars and is not adjusted for inflation or other time-dependent increases).[14]

5. Fill a capability gap as defined in the *BioWatch Gen–3 Mission Needs Statement* and align with (or have) a viable concept of operations.

---

[7] Ibid.

[8] DHS published an interim *Acquisition Directive 102–01* in November 2008; this document includes the requirement for a capability development plan "including the initial ground rules for the Analysis of Alternatives (AoA) or Alternatives Analysis (AA) . . . to begin the Analyze/ Select phase" once the Mission Needs Statement (MNS) is approved. DHS, Acquisition Directive 102–01, version 1.9, Interim (Washington, DC: DHS, 2008), 14.

[9] DHS, *Acquisition Management Directive 102–01* (hereafter: AMD 102–01) (Washington, DC: DHS, 2010), 6; this document has since been supplemented and collated into DHS, *Acquisition Management Directive 102–01,* Revision 2 (hereafter: AMD 102–01 Rev. 2) (Washington, DC: DHS, 2013).

[10] DHS, *Mission Needs Statement for BioWatch Gen–3 Autonomous Detection System* (hereafter: *Mission Needs Statement v.2.0*), Version 2.0, DRAFT (Washington, DC: DHS, 2012), FOUO.

[11] "Department of Homeland Security Research & Development Partnerships Group: Product Realization Guide," DHS, accessed January 7, 2013, *https://www.dhs.gov/sites/default/files/ publications/product-realization-guide-partnership-focus-508-1.pdf.* Technology readiness level 6 indicates that the capability of a representative model or prototype system has been tested in a relevant environment, including a laboratory or simulated operational environment. Taken from: Homeland Security Institute, *Department of Homeland Security Science and Technology Readiness Level Calculator,* Version 1.1 (Washington, DC: Homeland Security Institute, 2009), B–23.

[12] This is based on the stated assumption that a BioWatch Gen–3 detector will be available and fielded within 2 to 5 years.

[13] DHS, *BioWatch Gen–3 Systems Engineering Life Cycle Tailoring (SELCT) Plan for the BioWatch Generation–3 Program, Version 1.1* (Washington, DC: DHS/OHA, 2012), A–1, FOUO; and DHS/OHA, *Gen–3 ORD,* 3–1, FOUO.

[14] In the final evaluation of alternatives, budget should be a constraint and is, therefore, listed here. Budget, however, is not used as a hard boundary in this AoA because the exact BioWatch budget is not known. GAO, BioSurveillance—Reevaluate Mission Need, 26, 30–31; and, DHS, "BioWatch Gen–3 Phase II Industry Day," briefing, Washington, DC, September 12, 2011.

Based on these criteria, the IDA team proposed four alternatives for additional analyses. Additional analyses included casualty modeling, life-cycle cost estimates, and evaluation of the Net Present Value and Return on Investment.

2. Selected Alternative Biosurveillance Candidates

The four selected candidate alternatives identified through the AoA process and approved as reasonable capability representatives by the DHS Acting Principal Deputy Assistant Secretary of Health Affairs [15] are (in alphabetical order):

1. Autonomous Identification:[16] Autonomous and integrated multi-component systems that perform all environmental sampling and on-site testing without human intervention or control.

2. Clinical diagnosis/diagnostics with mandatory U.S. Centers for Disease Control and Prevention (CDC)/local public health disease reporting (hereafter Clinical Diagnosis/Diagnostics): Technologies and activities used in combination to evaluate and assess the disease manifesting in symptomatic individuals, combined with notification to the CDC regarding the detection of specific diseases in a timely manner.

3. Environmental collection with manual sample retrieval with analytical laboratory (hereafter Environmental Collection[17]): Technologies that collect aerosol samples that are manually retrieved and transported to an analytical laboratory for analysis.

4. Sentinel population with technological collectors with analytical laboratory (hereafter Sentinel Population): A limited portion of the population (e.g., law enforcement officers) wearing lightweight, portable, personal air samplers to collect samples for detection/identification of biological agents with subsequent laboratory analysis.

3. Metrics, Scenarios, and Assumptions

a. Mission Tasks, Measures of Effectiveness (MOE), and Measures of Performance (MOP)

Upon the selection of the four alternatives, the next step in the AoA process was to formulate a hierarchy of metrics including mission tasks, measures of effectiveness, and measures of performance.

Per *HSPD–10* and the BioWatch documentation, a BioWatch system has four specific mission tasks:[18]

- Early warning: Detect an aerosolized biological agent attack 24 hours per day, 365 days per year;
- Reinforce existing systems: Utilize concept of operations, processes, and other biosurveillance activities that have been accepted by Federal, State, and local authorities to evaluate a BioWatch Actionable Result (BAR);[19]
- Timely response: Identify a BioWatch actionable result and initiate an appropriate public health intervention in a timely manner; and
- Operate in Multiple Environments: Operate in outdoor, indoor, and mixed (indoor and outdoor) environments.

Based on the mission tasks, three measures of effectiveness were identified: (1) Availability—degree that a system or group of systems are operationally capable of performing an assigned mission;[20] (2) casualties—number of exposed and infected individuals who eventually manifest disease symptoms following a BioWatch actionable result and a subsequent trigger of a public health intervention,[21] estimated as a function of the systems' ability to respond within an allotted time and the speed

---

[15] Sally Phillips, "DHS Office of Health Affairs (OHA) Review of Candidates Selected for BioWatch Analysis of Alternatives (AoA)," memorandum to Deena Disraelly, May 24, 2013.

[16] Proposed as an autonomous detection platform, BioWatch Gen–3 would be an example of an autonomous identification capability.

[17] Environmental Collection simulates the current BioWatch Generation–2 system.

[18] Bush, *HSPD–10*, 6; DHS, *Mission Needs Statement v.2.0*, C–5, FOUO; and DHS/OHA, *SELCT Plan*, 3–4, FOUO.

[19] In this instance, the term BioWatch Actionable Result (BAR) denotes the positive presence of a biological threat agent in an environmental or clinical sample; for the purposes of this study, the BioWatch actionable result triggers a response in the form of a stakeholder meeting/teleconference to discern if a threat exists and determine what, if any, public health intervention is required.

[20] Defense Acquisition University, "Operational Availability," in *Glossary of Defense Acquisition Acronyms and Terms*, 15th ed., December 2012, accessed July 30, 2013, *https://dap.dau.mil/glossary/Pages/2331.aspx.*

[21] For each candidate alternative, casualties are calculated following a BioWatch actionable result, which triggers a public health intervention.

or delay between steps in a biosurveillance system;[22] and (3) probability of detection—effectiveness of the alternative at detecting aerosolized biological weapons attacks, measured using the probability of detection calculation as a proxy as described below.[23]

The IDA team then identified five measures of performance that were mapped to the measures of effectiveness (see Figure 1). These measures of performance included coverage, number of detectable and identifiable agents, operational environment, probability of detection, and time to detect/identify.

b. Operational and Modeling Scenarios

The four selected candidate alternatives were evaluated against three operational scenarios each with its own operational setting—outdoors (represented by metropolitan Chicago), indoors (represented by O'Hare International Airport, Chicago), and inside a transportation center (represented by Grand Central Terminal, New York). These scenarios were intended to replicate the scenarios outlined for BioWatch Gen–3 in its concept of operations document.[24] This evaluation used results derived from earlier modeling efforts conducted by Sandia National Laboratories (SNL) and Los Alamos National Laboratories (LANL), which represented attacks with three biothreat agents (Bacillus anthracis, Yersinia pestis, and Francisella tularensis)[25] and variable attack sizes, locations, and times of day.

The operational scenarios were modeled to determine the amount of time required to detect and identify an agent, the time to establish a point of distribution (POD) to begin dissemination of prophylaxis, the probability that a given alternative would detect an attack, and the number of casualties resulting from the attack. Figure 2 illustrates the modeling process used in this AoA. Life-cycle cost estimates were constructed independently for the four alternatives. Next, modeling and life-cycle cost estimates results were combined to evaluate Net Present Value and Return on Investment.[26]

c. Assumptions

Several assumptions were included in the modeling process. They are as follows:
1. Each biological surveillance alternative capability can be assessed independently or in combination with other capabilities.
2. Three diseases—anthrax, plague, and tularemia—are assumed to be representative of the diseases in the BioWatch Gen–3 operational requirements document (ORD).
3. Biological exposure and contagious spread (if any) are restricted and limited to specific geographical location/region where the release occurred.
4. A BioWatch Gen–3 autonomous biological agent detector would be available for deployment in 2 to 5 years.
5. One biological identification is a BioWatch actionable result.
6. Casualty estimates are given in days (rather than hours) to avoid implying a higher level of precision than is supported by the relevant literature.
7. Notional classes of capabilities are an appropriate representation of alternatives.
8. Timeliness of the response is a function of when the public health intervention occurs as defined by the antibiotic prophylaxis points of distribution being opened to the public.
9. Twenty-four hours is required from the decision to deploy the strategic National stockpile for antibiotic prophylaxis to the opening of the points of dis-

---

[22] Douglas N. Klaucke et al., "Guidelines for Evaluating Surveillance Systems," *Morbidity and Mortality Weekly Report (MMWR)* 37, no. S–5 (1988): 1–18; and Ruth A. Jajosky and Samuel L. Groseclose, "Evaluation of Reporting Timeliness of Public Health Surveillance Systems for Infectious Diseases," *BioMed Central (BMC) Public Health* 4, no. 29 (2004): 1–9.

[23] Nerayo P. Teclemariam et al., *BioWatch Technical Analysis of Biodetection Architecture Performance*, Sandia Report, SAND2012–0125 (Livermore, CA: Sandia National Laboratories, 2012), 16, FOUO.

[24] DHS, *Acquisition Concept of Operations (CONOPS) for BioWatch Gen–3* (Hereafter: *Acquisition CONOPS for Gen–3*), version 0.1 (Washington, DC: DHS, 2012), FOUO.

[25] Due to the diversity of these agents with regard to contagion, lethality, and long-term care requirements, these three diseases were considered representative of the diseases resulting from aerosolized exposure to the five threshold biological agents required for Gen–3.

[26] Net Present Value is the present value of calculated benefits and costs over a defined number of time periods—for the purpose of IDA's study, 20 years. Return on Investment is the net benefit expressed as a percentage of the investment amount. Net Present Value and Return on Investment may also be negative depending on perceived risk of attack and value of human life for three of the four alternatives. Clinical Diagnosis/Diagnostics always has a positive Net Present Value and Return on Investment.

tribution with an additional 24 hours to distribute the prophylaxis[27] for all candidate alternatives and excursions.

10. The study assumes that antibiotic prophylaxis is distributed to the entire population on the day the points of distribution open; prophylaxis is effective 1 day later.

11. The population is assumed to be 100% compliant in taking the directed course of antibiotic prophylaxis.

12. For the outdoor release, all individuals with a given aerosolized agent concentration at a given latitude and longitude receive the same exposure.[28]

13. Detections in a scenario are independent of any other nearby alternative employments (e.g., there are no outdoor detections for an indoor scenario).[29]

14. Casualties are evaluated as a function of exposure to a biological agent and the resulting symptomatic illness; mass casualty medical interventions are not included in the modeling.

15. Life-cycle cost estimate calculations are made in U.S. Government fiscal year 2013 dollars, with results presented at the 50% confidence level.[30]

16. Each year in the life-cycle cost estimate is based on the fiscal year, which runs from October 1 to September 30 and program costs are incurred beginning on October 1, 2013.

17. Estimates assume a 20-year operational life span beginning in fiscal year 2014 and ending in fiscal year 2033, with full implementation of material solutions by fiscal year 2018.

18. Material solutions were assumed to be deployed to 50 cities per the concept of operations for BioWatch Gen–3.[31]

19. The IDA team excluded the costs of construction/base operation of certain public health infrastructure, notably hospitals and analytical or clinical laboratory facilities.

20. Estimates do not include either the cost of patient treatment once a decision has been made to establish points of distribution for prophylaxis or the cost of remediation (e.g., facility decontamination).

21. Estimates include an information management system (IMS) that was developed and costed independent of each alternative.

22. The cost of decommissioning hardware is assumed to be similar for all material systems.

23. Unless otherwise noted, life-cycle cost estimates do not include the cost of equipment being further designed and developed using Government funds, assuming that solutions are fully developed and could be purchased from a vendor. Additionally, unless otherwise noted, test and evaluation costs are not included. Both these assumptions could increase life-cycle cost estimates.

D. AOA PROJECT FINDINGS

1. Modeling Findings

The biosensor alternatives—specifically Autonomous Identification, Environmental Collection, and the Sentinel Population alternative—would benefit from improved probability of detection. Probability of detection can be improved by either increasing the number of systems deployed (for the Autonomous Identification and Environmental Collection systems) or by increasing the sensitivity[32] of these systems. Improved probability of detection, however, may also increase system costs.

For the biosensor alternatives in an outdoor attack, probability of detection is approximately 50% or less for attacks that cause 100 or more casualties and 65% or less for 10,000 casualties. Indoors, probability of detection is greater, approaching 100% in those cases in which there are upwards of 10,000 casualties, resulting in less reliance on clinical diagnostics/diagnoses to trigger the distribution of prophylaxis.

---

[27] Mark Whitworth, *RSS Analysis Project Final Report* (Cambridge, MA: Center for Emergency Response Analytics, 2009), 7.

[28] Roebert L. Stearman, *Protection Against Chemical Attack Provided by Buildings,* Technical Report DPG–S–TA–85–05 (Dugway, UT: U.S. Army Dugway Proving Ground, 1985).

[29] The versions of the outdoor and indoor transport and dispersions models employed in this study to estimate agent concentrations were unable to exchange data between one another, making it very difficult to transfer agent concentrations from one domain to another.

[30] See footnote 1 in "Certification of Acquisition Funding" (memorandum from Peggy Sherry, Chief Financial Officer, to Component Senior Financial Officers, Department of Homeland Security, December 2, 2012).

[31] DHS, *Acquisition CONOPS for Gen–3,* 45–47, FOUO.

[32] System sensitivity is the amount of mass of agent required to be present in a sample for it to be identified by a detector or in a laboratory process.

In general, for attack scenarios modeled in this AoA:
- All four alternatives demonstrated approximately equivalent availability for aerosolized biological agent events: i.e., equivalent coverage of 50 (or more) cities; ability to detect the five threshold BioWatch agents or more; and capability to operate in a variety of environments.
- Autonomous Identification was consistently the quickest alternative to identify any of the three agents (at 6 hours), followed by the Sentinel Population alternative (generally at 18 hours), Environmental Collection (at 34 hours), and Clinical Diagnosis/Diagnostics (at 4–13 days, depending on the agent). Timeliness is illustrated in Figure 3.
- Clinical Diagnosis/Diagnostics has the highest probability of detection (i.e., all agents will ultimately be detected) for both indoor and outdoor scenarios.
  - Environmental Collection and the Sentinel Population alternative approach 99% detection indoors depending on the scenario.
  - The probability of detection for Environmental Collection and the Sentinel Population alternatives is less than 50% for the outdoor scenario; for Autonomous Identification, it is less than 25%.
  - More detail on the probability of detection results are in Figure 4.
- For detected attacks, Autonomous Identification and Sentinel Population alternatives lead to the fewest casualties, followed by Environmental Collection and Clinical Diagnosis/Diagnostics, though the magnitude of differences between alternatives tends to be agent-dependent. Given the high concentrations found in the indoor scenarios, resulting in the more rapid onset of severe disease symptoms, the biosensor alternatives were less effective at reducing casualties for the indoor scenarios.
- These casualty results are illustrated for anthrax and plague in Figure 5.

Several factors have the potential to change these findings. They include sensor sensitivity, number of sensors deployed, number of detections required to initiate a public health intervention, frequency of sampling, new diagnostic protocols/tools, leadership's willingness to act, different concept of operations and employment, and human behavior. There are also several non-quantified considerations that should be kept in mind, including false positive rates, situational awareness and characterization, rapidly confirmable information, possibility of exposure limitation through facility closure (indoor scenario), and the availability of forensic samples (wet or dry).

2. Cost Findings

Life-cycle cost estimates were developed based on the major cost drivers for selected candidate alternatives over the 20-year life span. The Sentinel Population alternative has the highest life-cycle costs, roughly an order of magnitude higher than Autonomous Identification and Environmental Collection, which are approximately equivalent. Clinical Diagnosis/Diagnostics, which assumes a pre-existing public health infrastructure and includes only the costs of testing (not treating) a small population of patients and the deployment of an information management system, is the lowest-cost alternative. The life-cycle cost estimates are illustrated in Figure 6, with Clinical Diagnosis/Diagnostics as the least expensive option at approximately $43 million. Sentinel Population was the most expensive option ($16.4 billion). Environmental Collection and Autonomous Identification were estimated at $3.7 and $4.2 billion respectively.

Cost-effectiveness was evaluated by comparing cost against a variety of effectiveness measures. Life-cycle cost estimates were compared to the probability of detection, the casualties for a number of representative attacks, and the detection-adjusted casualties.[33] The Sentinel Population alternative often achieves the lowest detection adjusted casualties value, owing to its high probability of rapid detection and high cost due to its large number of samples. Conversely, although Clinical Diagnosis/Diagnostics has the highest probability of detection, the relatively long time before a detection can be obtained (and therefore extended time before antibiotic prophylaxis can be administered), results in the highest detection adjusted casualties value. Environmental Collection and Autonomous Identification are roughly equivalent in terms of cost and detection adjusted casualties for most scenarios.

E. CONCLUDING REMARKS

The principal BioWatch AoA findings are:

---

[33] Detection-adjusted casualties estimates the expected number of casualties as a function of the probability of detection. It is a weighted average of casualties that occur when there is a detection and when there is no detection.

- Any biosurveillance solution involves a combination of material and non-material capabilities as well as defined doctrine and procedures to facilitate decisions by local and State leadership, and public health, law enforcement, emergency management, public works, transportation, and other public and private stakeholders.
- Improved probability of detection for the biosensor alternatives options will result in earlier detection and decreased casualties and, therefore, lower detection-adjusted casualties.
- Autonomous Identification, Clinical Diagnosis/Diagnostics, and Environmental Collection were all below the life-cycle cost constraint of $5.8 billion (as cited by the GAO).[34] The Sentinel Population alternative exceeds the constraint due to the high number of deployed collectors and the associated laboratory and processing requirements.
- The selected candidate alternatives were evaluated against a variety of metrics. These findings, as summarized in Figure 7, present a number of criteria which could, independently or in combination, inform future BioWatch discussions.

The choice of alternative (whether Autonomous Identification, Clinical Diagnosis/Diagnostics, Environmental Collection or a combination) depends on a variety of system factors, as well as factors with the potential to assist and influence decision makers using BioWatch system information. Table 1 shows several criteria that DHS might consider, independently or in combination, when selecting a BioWatch alternative and the corresponding system potentially best suited (given each criteria) for systems deployed outdoors, indoors, and in combined environments.

There is a positive Net Present Value and Return on Investment for each of the four alternatives, depending on the perceived risk of attack and value associated with a human life. Clinical Diagnosis/Diagnostics is the least expensive alternative with the highest probability of detection but also is likely to result in the highest number of casualties due to delays in disease detection and identification. Indoors, both Autonomous Identification and Environmental Collection have roughly equivalent detection adjusted casualties values. Autonomous Identification shows reductions in casualties as compared with Clinical Diagnosis/Diagnostics for detected attacks due to the system's timeliness of warning, while delays in warning for Environmental Collection are ameliorated by its higher probability of detection.[35] Outdoors, Environmental Collection has the lowest detection adjusted casualties due to its higher probability of detection as compared to Autonomous Identification and its timeliness as compared to Clinical Diagnosis/Diagnostics.

Insofar as there is a requirement for earlier warning and detection, employing a biosensor system according to a planned concept of operations—with appropriate response by decision-making authorities and timely engagement by public health officials—would yield fewer casualties and potentially non-quantifiable benefits, including forensic samples, rapidly confirmable information, situational awareness and characterization, and improved planning and preparedness.

Homeland Security Presidential Directive (HSPD)–10, BioDefense for the 21st Century states:

"Early warning, detection, or recognition of biological weapons attacks to permit a timely response to mitigate their consequences is an essential component of biodefense . . . creating a national bioawareness system will permit the recognition of a biological attack at the earliest possible moment and permit initiation of a robust response to prevent unnecessary loss of life, economic losses, and social disruption."[36]

HSPD–10 is still in effect. This directive requires DHS to maintain a detection and early warning system. This Analysis of Alternatives provided DHS with information with which to evaluate alternate approaches to providing that capability.

---

[34] "In June 2011, DHS provided a risk-adjusted estimate at the 80 percent confidence level of $5.8 billion [2010 dollars];" GAO, *BioSurveillance—Reevaluate Mission Need,* 3.

[35] It is important to remember that the AoA used Gen–3 ORD values for Autonomous Identification sensitivity rather than a specific system data as no representative system has yet been selected. Demonstrated improvements in system sensitivity beyond those required in the Gen–3 ORD improve the system probability of detection and detection adjusted casualties as discussed in Section 6.

[36] Bush, *HSPD–10,* 6.

Referenced Figures and Tables

		Probability of Detection (Pd)	Casualties	Availability
Mission Tasks	Detect 24/7/365	X		X
	Timely response		X	
	Multiple environments			X
	CONOPS to evaluate a BAR			X
MOEs		Probability of Detection (Pd)	Casualties	Availability
MOPs	Coverage			X
	Number of detectable and identifiable agents			X
	Operational environment			X
	Probability of detection	X		
	Time to detect		X	
	Time to identify		X	

Figure 1. Mapping Mission Tasks, Measures of Effectiveness (MOE), and Measures of Performance (MOP)

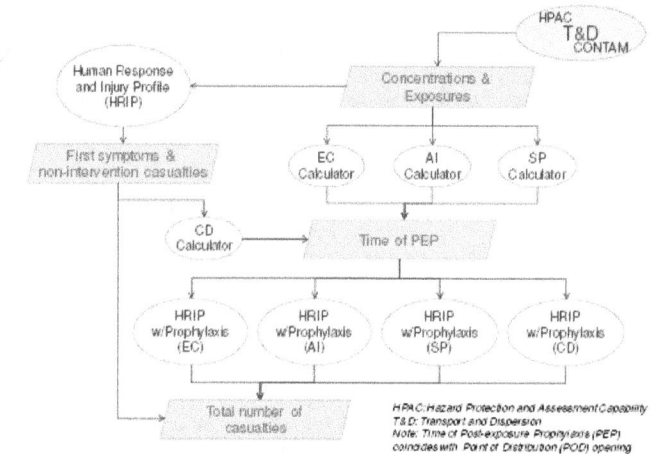

Note: AI = Autonomous Identification; CD = Clinical Diagnosis/Diagnostics; EC = Environmental Collection; SP = Sentinel Population alternative.

Figure 2. Modeling Process Flow

Time to Agent Detection & Identification (BAR): Alternative	Anthrax	Plague	Tularemia
Autonomous Identification	6 hours		
Environmental Collection	34 hours		
Sentinel Population	18-26 hours	18 hours	
Clinical Diagnosis	4 days	5 days	13 days

BioWatch Actionable Result (BAR):
A BAR is defined as "one or more polymerase chain reaction (PCR)-verified positive result(s) from a single BioWatch collector that meets the algorithm for one or more specific BioWatch agents."

Base Case: Agent release at beginning of collection cycle

- Autonomous Identification: 4 hour collection/ 2 hour processing
- Environmental Collection: 28 hour collection/ 6 hour processing
- Sentinel Population: 50% tested outdoor; 12 hour collection/6 hour processing
- Clinical Diagnosis: Test at fulminant stage; 3 hour collection/24 hour processing

Collection cycle: sample collection, manual collection & transport

Time of PEP Administration: Alternative	Anthrax	Plague	Tularemia
Autonomous Identification	2 days	2 days	2 days
Environmental Collection	3 days	3 days	3 days
Sentinel Population	2-3 days	2 days	2 days
Clinical Diagnosis	5 days	6 days	14 days

Figure 3. Modeling—Timeliness, Base Case

Alternative (Probability of detection for attacks causing >100 casualties)	Chicago Outdoor			O'Hare Airport			Grand Central Terminal		
	Anthrax	Plague	Tularemia	Anthrax	Plague	Tularemia	Anthrax	Plague	Tularemia
Autonomous Identification	23%	23%	23%	45%	42%	40%	82%	77%	77%
Environmental Collection	42%	41%	41%	65%	65%	61%	99%	99%	99%
Sentinel Population	44%	42%	46%	92%	91%	90%	99%	99%	99%
Clinical Diagnosis	100%	100%	100%	100%	100%	100%	100%	100%	100%

Note: Probability of detection for attacks causing greater than 10,000 casualties rapidly approaches 99% for indoor locations.

Sources: Nerayo P. Teclemariam et al., *BioWatch Technical Analysis of Biodetection Architecture Performance*, Sandia Report, SAND2012-0125 (Livermore: Sandia National Laboratories, 2012), FOUO; and IDA modeling work as documented in Disraelly et al., *BioWatch Analysis of Alternatives*, Institute for Defense Analyses (IDA) Paper P-5083 (Alexandria, VA: IDA, 2013).

Figure 4. Modeling—Probability of Detection

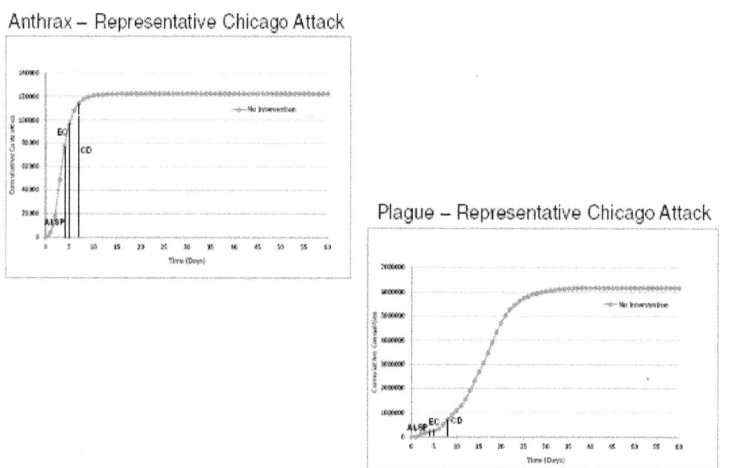

Note: AI = Autonomous Identification; CD = Clinical Diagnosis/Diagnostics; EC = Environmental Collection;
SP = Sentinel Population alternative.

Figure 5. Modeling—Casualties Over Time, Base Case

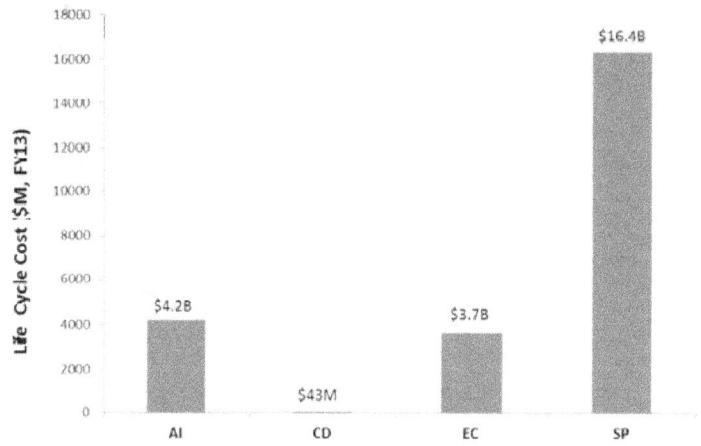

Note: AI = Autonomous Identification; CD = Clinical Diagnosis/Diagnostics; EC = Environmental Collection;
SP = Sentinel Population alternative.

Figure 6. Cost Estimation—Life Cycle Cost Estimate Summary ($M, FY13, 50% Risk
Adjusted)

MOEs & MOPs/ Alternatives	EC	AI	SP	CD
Availability	Approximately equivalent for aerosolized biological agent events			
Coverage	50 cities	50 cities	50 cities	Cities w/hospital lab capability
Detectable and identifiable agents (fatality risk)	100%	100%	100%	100%
Operational environment	1	1	1	1
Probability of Detection	41-99%	23-82%	42-99%	100%
Casualties	Casualties are a function of agent & time to PEP administration, vary by attack			
Time to detect/identify	34 hours	6 hours	18-26 hours	4-13 days
Time to PEP Administration	3 days	2 days	2-3 days	5-14 days
Life Cycle Costs constrained at $5.8B (GAO 2012)				
	$3.7B	$4.2B	$16.4B	$43M

Note: AI = Autonomous Identification; CD = Clinical Diagnosis/Diagnostics; EC = Environmental Collection; SP = Sentinel Population alternative; PEP = Post-exposure Prophylaxis.

Figure 7. Alternatives versus Measures of Effectiveness, Measures of Performance

	Combined[2]	Outdoors	Indoors
Detection Adjusted Casualties	not applicable[3]	EC	AI/EC
Probability of detection	CD[4]	CD[4]	CD[4]
Casualties	AI	AI	AI
Timeliness	AI	AI	AI
Cost[5]		CD[4]	

Table 1. Selected Candidate Alternatives under Various BioWatch Selection Criteria[1]

Note: AI = Autonomous Identification; CD = Clinical Diagnostics/Diagnosis; EC = Environmental Collection; SP = Sentinel Population alternative.

[1] The cost of the Sentinel Population alternative is well above any cited BioWatch budget figure and therefore is considered outside the study constraints; subsequently, the Sentinel Population alternative is not considered in the table.

[2] The combined environment is one that includes co-located indoor and outdoor spaces (e.g., transportation facilities, stadiums).

[3] The modeling data did not allow for modeling of a release in a combined environment, or a mixed indoors and outdoors transportation environment, therefore, the exact number of casualties, probability of detection, and detection adjusted casualties could not be modeled.

[4] The findings shown above for Clinical Diagnosis/Diagnostics consider only the current use and existing or mass casualty protocols; any change in systems, number of diagnostic samples, and protocols would require a reevaluation of the alternative's utility and costs.

[5] Cost was assessed for the complete deployment of material and non-material solutions across all locations. Therefore, the most cost-effective solution is shown at left.

Mrs. BROOKS. Thank you, Dr. Disraelly.

The Chairwoman will now recognize myself for 5 minutes of questioning. I will recognize other Members of the subcommittee for questions they may wish to ask the witnesses.

In accordance with our committee rules, I plan to recognize Members who were present at the start of the hearing by seniority on the subcommittee. Those coming in later will be recognized in the order of their arrival.

I would like to just confirm with everyone, or particularly, actually, with Dr. Brinsfield, Dr. Brothers, and Dr. Disraelly, do you think—simple yes or no—that bioterrorism continues to be a significant threat about which this Nation needs to be concerned? Yes or no? That is all I want to know. Dr. Brinsfield.

Dr. BRINSFIELD. Yes, we continue to be concerned.

Mrs. BROOKS. Dr. Brothers.

Mr. BROTHERS. Yes.

Mrs. BROOKS. Dr. Disraelly.

Ms. DISRAELLY. Yes.

Mrs. BROOKS. With a yes or no, do you believe, what you know now, that the Gen–2 system is sufficient? Yes or no? Dr. Brinsfield.

Dr. BRINSFIELD. We believe the Gen–2 system works. We believe that a Gen–3 system would—or another system that did autonomous detection could be an improvement in the future.

Mrs. BROOKS. Okay. Dr. Brothers.

Mr. BROTHERS. Agree. I believe we get effectiveness from the Gen–2 system and believe we could have some improved capabilities with a Gen–3 system.

Mrs. BROOKS. Dr. Disraelly.

Ms. DISRAELLY. We believe that environmental collection is a viable alternative and that with improvements autonomous identification may be, as well.

Mrs. BROOKS. Okay. Thank you. As I noted in my opening statement, the administration did release its National Biosurveillance Survey—Strategy rather in July 2012, and we are now coming up on 2 years and we have yet, as Mr. Currie noted, the plan for implementation of this important strategy was to be completed in the fall 2012.

To date that plan has yet to be completed. It seems as if we have a National strategy but yet we have no implementation plan as to how to implement the strategy, that there has not been sufficient attention being driven to this problem.

Dr. Brinsfield, can you share with us, having served on National Security Staff and now in your capacity, can you shed any light when this plan will be completed? If you could, please share with us what has caused this delay.

Dr. BRINSFIELD. I think this plan—it would be honest to say that our staff is working diligently with the staff at the NSC right now. There is a rapid pace to this implementation plan's development, and I have good faith that when it is released it will be a good plan and incorporate all the necessary elements.

Mrs. BROOKS. What has taken 2 years?

Dr. BRINSFIELD. I don't think you could really say any one particular issue. I think it is important to make sure that you get all the different partners and agencies to the table and make sure that we have the right expertise and look at this data, the science. So I am very pleased with the progress it is making.

Mrs. BROOKS. How many people are working on the plan?

Dr. BRINSFIELD. On a regular basis in meetings, the meetings tend to be 10 to 20 people big. It depends. There are a lot of departments and agencies that participate. We have staff members that participate on a regular basis.

Mrs. BROOKS. When can we anticipate the completion of the plan? In 2014?

Dr. BRINSFIELD. Ma'am, I can't answer that question, but I will be glad to work to get back to you.

Mrs. BROOKS. Who is in charge of it?

Dr. BRINSFIELD. That would be at the National Security Staff for final release.

Mrs. BROOKS. So who is in charge of it? Who is in charge?

Dr. BRINSFIELD. Of the National Security Staff?

Mrs. BROOKS. No, of the—who is responsible for ensuring there is an implementation plan that is developed?

Dr. BRINSFIELD. Ma'am, I will get back to you. I don't want to speak to their activities. I will get back to you with an answer, if I may.

Mrs. BROOKS. Dr. Brothers, do you know?

Mr. BROTHERS. I do not have an answer for that. Glad to work with Dr. Brinsfield to come up with an answer.

Mrs. BROOKS. With respect to the Quadrennial Homeland Security Review—and this is for Dr. Brinsfield and Dr. Brothers—the 2014 Homeland Security review includes a review of the biological threat landscape that we have reviewed and the Department's strategy to counter these threats. It was—the Quadrennial Review was due to Congress by December 21, 2013. Do we have any idea when that will be submitted to Congress, Dr. Brinsfield or Dr. Brothers?

Dr. BRINSFIELD. I am sorry, ma'am. Can you repeat the last part of the question?

Mrs. BROOKS. When the 2014 Quadrennial Homeland Security Review, it was due to Congress end of 2013, but we have yet to see it. Are you familiar with this report?

Dr. BRINSFIELD. Very familiar, ma'am, and that is why I was trying to make sure I understood correctly. Maybe Mr. Cummiskey can answer to the exact date of its release, but very familiar with the report and its finding.

Mr. CUMMISKEY. Chairwoman Brooks, I understand that the QHSR is forthcoming. It should be here shortly in the not-too-distant future. I can't give you a precise day, but it is intended to be here in the next 7 to 10 days.

Mrs. BROOKS. Thank you. Will it address biothreats in the report? Do we anticipate that biothreats will be addressed in the report?

Dr. BRINSFIELD. Yes ma'am, it does.

Mrs. BROOKS. Okay. Thank you. We look forward to that. My time is up.

Mr. PAYNE. Thank you, Madam Chairwoman. Excuse me.

This question is for Dr. Brinsfield and Dr. Brothers as well. You know, after DHS canceled the Gen–3 acquisition, the Secretary directed the Office of Health Affairs and Science and Technology Directorate to complete two reports within 2 weeks of the April 2014 ADM.

One report is to address lessons learned and the other is to lay out a strategy moving forward. It has been a month-and-a-half since the decision to discontinue Gen–3 was announced. What is the status of those reports requested by the Secretary and why have the documents been delayed?

Dr. BRINSFIELD. We have been working very closely on those documents. We have actually submitted those documents for Department review.

Mr. PAYNE. Okay. Can you give us an idea or sense of the major findings or strategies that will be included?

Dr. BRINSFIELD. I think in the first report that looked at history, I would concur with much of what has been discussed here today. We looked at how information is generated, requirements are generated, looking forward to a coordinated process in that effect.

Also looked at how the acquisition process moves forward and how we can make sure that the best decisions are being made. In the second report, I will defer in a second to Dr. Brothers, but I think what we have agreed to is looking together in a collaborative fashion at how we can move forward in the technology space.

Mr. BROTHERS. Yes. I think we have talked to kind-of a near-term and a far-term look at this. Where in near-term we are looking at what we can do to augment the current system. Then in the far-term what we can do to look at increased capabilities, maybe distributed, a sensor-agnostic type-of system. So we are working together to try to flesh those things out.

Mr. PAYNE. Okay. Dr. Disraelly, in your testimony you note that the IDA team identified about 500 technologies that are either readily-deployable or in development, and that ultimately you narrowed it down, the available technologies, to four for purposes of the AOA. Can you talk about some of the technologies that were not selected to be considered for the AOA and why?

Ms. DISRAELLY. The 500 technologies and capabilities that we included, or that we mentioned, included activities, programs, and technologies themselves. We sorted those into 29 classes of capabilities. So basically like was sorted with like.

One example of a technology, for example, that was not included was social media. Social media gets a lot of attention right now as an epidemiological tool and a tracking tool in the public health sector.

However, people aren't reporting on social media until after they have actually been diagnosed with a disease, and therefore it doesn't have the timeliness factor that clinical diagnosis and diagnostics does because we would already know that the disease was present, before social media actually was able find it. Does that give you an answer?

Mr. PAYNE. Okay. Let's see. In terms of the GAO, Dr. Brinsfield, they observed that the National Academy of Sciences has raised questions about the effectiveness of the currently deployed Gen–2 BioWatch system. You know, other critics have raised concerns regarding whether Gen–2 addresses the threats raised by our intelligence community. Members of this panel have historically raised similar concerns.

What efforts will you take to examine and reevaluate the concerns as you consider replacing Gen–2 equipment? We know that it was stated this morning already that some of that equipment is coming to the end of its life cycle or its usefulness. I think technology has moved dramatically in terms of what is possible in this area since Gen–2 was implemented. So could you speak to that?

Dr. BRINSFIELD. Sure. I will speak briefly and then turn it over again. First, to the question of does the current system work, we have data analyzing its current effectiveness that we would be happy to share with the committee environment, if you would like us to come back.

In terms of future threats, I think exactly as Dr. Brothers was saying, as we look at the future technology we want to make sure that it covers a broader array and that we think broadly about what the current risks are.

Mr. BROTHERS. Yes. I mean, I think some of the fundamental things we are looking at going forward are getting greater confidence in our systems so that the leadership has to make decisions of what to do when these events happen that they have greater confidence in the answers. A shorter time frame, because I think we were talking earlier about casualty rates and the importance of early detection.

So those are some of the things we are looking at. Whether we go from signature detection to more anomaly detection, there are different ways of thinking about the problem and we will be looking at all of those.

Mr. PAYNE. From what I understand is that you would need a large aerosol pathogen to go through the system in order to detect it. What if you had a lone wolf-type situation? Would the system be able to capture that? Then the collection time is something that we need to consider, 24 to 36 hours before we could collect and identify that there is an issue. That is a pretty lengthy amount of time.

Dr. BRINSFIELD. Yes. I think we are going to look at all those issues as we move forward, both shortening the collection time, increasing the number of agents, and looking at different environments, whether it is just a broad aerosol environment, an indoor environment or other types of environments. We might want to do a collection. All of these are questions that have been looked at and raised and will be good questions to work together on going forward.

Mr. PAYNE. Okay. Well I hope, you know, based on where we are and the technology that we can—you know, we are starting all over. We have been working on I guess the Gen–3 really since 2003 maybe. So it is about a decade, and now we are going back to the drawing board.

It is very disturbing to have that situation arise now and knowing that the technology that we are using—I mean, if we started looking at Gen–3 a decade ago, then, you know, what does it say of Gen–2 and where it started? You know, we need to really find a way to get moving in terms of the technology before we have a calamity occur.

I will yield back. Sorry.

Mrs. BROOKS. Thank you.

At this time the Chairwoman now recognizes Vice Chair of the committee, the gentleman from Mississippi, Mr. Palazzo, for 5 minutes of questioning.

Mr. PALAZZO. Thank you, Madam Chairwoman.

Secretary Cummiskey, the Department has had a number of failed acquisitions over the course of its relatively short existence, SBInet, Emerge, and the ASP program, and now Gen–3. I applaud the Secretary for canceling a program that was not working.

What have we learned from each of these failed acquisitions that will help us avoid similar mistakes in the future, and what policies have you put in place to ensure more robust acquisition oversight?

Mr. CUMMISKEY. Thank you, Congressman.

We have taken a number of steps over the last several years to strengthen the entire life-cycle continuum. We started with oversight because that the area where we are already working with 123 other major acquisitions in the Department.

So what we have tried to do is strengthen that by creating the program acquisition and risk management entity within management, which is the acquisition oversight arm. We created the chief acquisition executive process in each of the components in order to make sure that they are invested in this or working in concert with the folks that are actually operators on the ground that are deploying these systems.

We have also worked closely on strengthening life-cycle cost estimating by shifting that function out of harm, the program accountability group, into the chief finance office of the Department so that we can get stronger life-cycle cost estimates in that oversight bucket.

The Secretary has called for a Unity of Effort in this area and so what we are doing is we are shifting our focus now to strategies and plans as well as joint capabilities and requirements development so that when you are feeding the oversight piece, we have got stronger pieces of the continuum, which we are going to reduce the likelihood that would be less successful.

Mr. PALAZZO. Okay. So you said you are going to continue to refine your acquisition oversight framework as a part of the Unity of Effort.

Can you elaborate on some of the things that you are refining now?

Mr. CUMMISKEY. Absolutely.

Congressman, first of all, let me thank the entire House and particularly the committee for the leadership on 4228. That piece of legislation will go a long way in codifying many of the things that we have tried to put into place in the oversight function.

What the Secretary is saying is that in terms of looking at the requirements, we have got to take a joint requirements perspective on this and not just have one component or office, you know, trying to develop that. So what he has called for is the development of a joint requirements council, which, again, I think the full committee has called for in the past, which would give us an opportunity to sit together and look at best practices in the space, strengthen the joint requirements so that when we are feeding the resourcing piece, we will have a better sense of what we are actually buying and increase the likelihood of success.

Mr. PALAZZO. Now both DOD and DHS S&T have been studying and developing environmental detection systems for some time.

Before deciding to begin the development of Gen–3 systems, did the BioWatch Program look at these existing systems and if so, what type of analysis was done to determine that BioWatch needed to develop its own technology? Can any of these systems be leveraged now to make improvements to the current system?

That is for Dr. Brinsfield, Dr. Brothers, and Mr. Cummiskey.

45

Dr. BRINSFIELD. So there was an integrated planning team that did meet in the early stages of this that included other departments and agencies providing input.

I will note that as of now, the Department of Defense is actually using some of the current Gen–3 equipment to test against their current system so we hope to have that information.

Mr. BROTHERS. I think that we have a good relationship with the Department of Defense. I think we look forward to leveraging those to work together in fielding the best system possible.

Mr. CUMMISKEY. Congressman, to be candid with you, we went back into some of the documentation that was essential to launch this successfully. It was not there. We had to go back and do the AOA, the other documentation around operational requirements and things of that nature.

So what we have done now is for the last 3 years, no program has advanced without making sure we are hitting those gates in concurrence with what the GAO has called for. So we are in a better position. We would anticipate going forward that all of that will be in place for Gen–3.

Mr. PALAZZO. Thank you.

I yield back.

Mrs. BROOKS. Thank you.

At this time, the Chairwoman now recognizes the gentleman from South Carolina, Mr. Sanford, for 5 minutes' questioning.

Mr. SANFORD. Thank you.

It strikes me that you could have the greatest technology in the world but if you didn't have appropriate and proper human infrastructure to manage that technology, you would still have a very, very serious, even gaping security hole.

So with that in mind, I listen to your answers to the Chairwoman's questions, simple questions on implementation and your answer, Dr. Brinsfield, your answer, Dr. Brothers, was "I don't know, and I don't know."

It just strikes me that that is the kind of mismatch between technology whether talking Gen–2 or Gen–3 that is quantitative, real, in some cases, proven, in some cases, not proven with a human infrastructure, which I think has been a lot of people's beef with homeland security as you look at different GAO reports and what-not.

Let me just go back to that question one more time because the Chairwoman asked, I thought, a fairly basic question on implementation. Why wouldn't you know?

Dr. BRINSFIELD. So, sir, I think we do a lot of work and work very hard with our State and local partners to make sure that both the BioWatch Program and the NBIC are very well-integrated with their strategies and where they are moving forward. I think the important thing to focus on here is the amount of time and effort we give to supporting the boots on the ground and the people that have to actually do the response, the first responders——

Mr. SANFORD. If I could respectfully interject, I have actually sat in that role and at a State level. A lot of times, we were driven by Federal mandates in terms of different benchmarks that they had laid out with regard to level of implementation.

So I mean, I had 8 years of experience in that particular regard. So respectfully I would disagree.

Is there integration? Absolutely. But in many cases, we were responding at the State level to what the Feds had laid out in terms of benchmarks. I don't understand why there wouldn't be, at least, benchmarks, at a minimum, benchmarks with regard to implementation to the Chairwoman's question.

Dr. BRINSFIELD. So I am very interested in hearing your perspective, and I would like to offer to get together and discuss this with you in the future. I think anything we could do to improve those relationships would be a good thing.

Mr. SANFORD. But that is still not answering the question on implementation.

Dr. BRINSFIELD. For implementation in terms of the strategy to move antibiotics into an area after release, there is a program within the CDC that measures that and does a very good job working with States and locals to provide benchmarks and measure that.

In terms of BioWatch, we have a very active group that is working on CONOPS with the State and locals both for outdoor and indoor monitoring to provide those benchmarks.

Mr. SANFORD. Again, respectfully, one of the things I often times say to my staff is, look, fewer words, more facts.

I guess I would put this in the same category. I am getting a lot of process but still no benchmarks in terms of the question the Chairwoman asked, which was, "Is there not any date specific in terms of the implementation"?

Dr. BRINSFIELD. You are asking on an implementation plan date release, which is an interagency process. Sir, I apologize but I can't give you a hard date on an interagency document.

Mr. SANFORD. But a ballpark?

Dr. BRINSFIELD. I would hope it would be released in the near future, sir. I know we are working very hard towards that end.

Mr. SANFORD. Any further illumination from your—do you understand my frustration? It just seems like it is what people hate most about Government, which is process, process, process, and process, with no sort of—okay.

I mean, I think that one of the things that people really admire about the military and the disjunction between the times where the military is perceived and where Homeland Security is perceived is that they will flat out give you a target. This is what we hope to do by this date. This is what we hope to do by this date. This is what we hope to do by this date.

They may or may not hit those benchmarks, but they will give you at least what they are shooting for. What I am hearing from your end is it is a process, and we are in that process. I think people find that very, very frustrating.

With that, I yield back.

Mrs. BROOKS. Thank you. Kind of building on that a little bit, I would like to—Mr. Currie, you talked about the fact that GAO found that, at least in 2012, DHS had no policies for defining and coordinating R&D. There are a lot of different groups within Homeland Security, and we have some new leaders here in Dr. Brinsfield and Dr. Brothers.

Can you share with us what GAO's recommendations were with respect to coordinating and the fact that all the technology, and I know it takes a lot to develop technology, but then to transfer it into implementation, but S&T had had no tech transfer that was successful. So what would we say should be happening within DHS?

Then I would like to go to Dr. Brinsfield and Dr. Brothers for more clarification about how you now are going to coordinate this plan so that we, as a country, and we as Congress can have more comfort than we do right now, that there is real technology R&D discussions and real implementation with respect to bioterrorism, which is very real and we have very great concerns about what is not happening.

Mr. Currie.

Mr. CURRIE. Thank you, Chairwoman Brooks.

You are correct. In 2012, we reported that DHS had no policies for coordinating or really managing its R&D investments, not just within S&T but across all the components. I liken the R&D situation at DHS to what the acquisition situation was at DHS probably 8 or 10 years ago when there were no acquisition policies.

The Department, as Mr. Cummiskey has outlined, has taken many steps to outline that they have new policies and practices for following those.

In R&D they have gotten a little bit of a late start on that. It is very similar. So let me give you an example of that. For example, a couple of years ago DHS had no definition for what R&D at the Department was. Other agencies like DOD or NASA use technology readiness levels and other things to define R&D. DHS did not have a common definition.

So——

Mrs. BROOKS. Would you agree—just to interrupt briefly—that in any development of anything new, the R&D costs, thereby the costs to the taxpayers, are often the highest in the R&D process?

Mr. CURRIE. Well, it is true. It costs a lot to research and develop technologies. But it is why we think it is very important and what we recommended is that they develop these policies for what R&D is going to look like through the life cycle, what S&T is going to do, but more importantly, what is going to happen when they transfer it to the components, and when is that going to happen?

I think on this issue we are talking about today, on BioWatch and biodetection, it is going to be very important that very early on S&T and NAFSA health affairs agree very early what is going to actually happen, what both parties are going to do, and when that transfer is going to occur.

Mrs. BROOKS. Thank you.

So, with that, Dr. Brinsfield and Dr. Brothers, I have tremendous respect for your qualifications for the offices that you are both holding and with your experience. So can you please share with us— and I applaud the Secretary's unity of effort charge—how is it going to work?

Mr. BROTHERS. So let me start off with one of the comments that was just made. We do actually have an R&D definition now. So I think that is very helpful. Because as you mentioned, without hav-

48

ing that kind of definition, it is very difficult to try to understand what we are talking about, right?

But we now do have a definition. You mentioned the NASA and DOD TRL, technology readiness level, way of looking at it. That is exactly the type of thing we have adopted. So we have the same kind of 6–1 to 6–7 type-of designation the Department of Defense does.

So that is going to be very helpful in us actually understanding what is going on across the Department.

The other piece here that is important to think about is in the 6 weeks that I have been there, I have made a point to actually— meeting with the component leads to try to understand what their needs are and also what is going on. I am in the process of that right now.

Part of this process of working with Dr. Brinsfield is understanding exactly the types of activities we have going on and what we should be doing going forward, as well.

So I think I mentioned earlier that there is this emphasis on near-term versus far-term. So particular to BioWatch is there will be a near-term effort that we will be looking at, trying to understand what we can do with existing capabilities, how we are going to augment those. There is a longer-term effort, as well.

I think I also mentioned that from an S&T perspective we are looking at doing a potential apex program to really try to figure out how we can push this technology.

But I think going back to this point of coordinating S&T, I think the roots—the basis of being able to do that is this definition and communication and collaboration with the component heads. That is part of what the Secretary's Unity of Effort call to action is all about.

So I am very confident that we can do this going forward.

Mrs. BROOKS. Dr. Brinsfield.

Dr. BRINSFIELD. We have already had numerous conversations about sort-of the big picture where we see this going forward. I think it is a good relationship. We are working well together. The staffs are working well together. I look forward to a structured joint requirements process. I think this will help to answer much of the issues.

Mrs. BROOKS. Dr. Disraelly, have you been consulted in—with respect to your report by OHA and by S&T on what your analysis was and what the alternatives were that your Institute has presented?

Ms. DISRAELLY. At several points during the study, all the way from its inception, all the way through its conclusion, we briefed several members of the Department of Homeland Security.

We had a stakeholder team that included nine organizations within the Department who were given the opportunity to participate in the briefings as well as comment on the documents as we went through.

Mrs. BROOKS. Did you feel that they were high-level individuals within DHS that participated? Or do there need to be additional meetings with respect to all of the work that your organization did?

Have you met with Dr. Brothers?

Ms. DISRAELLY. We have met with Dr. Brinsfield. The study was concluded before Dr. Brothers came to the Department, and so we have not briefed with him.

Mrs. BROOKS. Okay. I am certainly hopeful that all the work and I appreciate that you are new, but that collaboration can—with the analysis that has already been done, because it seems as though you are stepping into an organization that has not had much success in its tech transfer and in its implementation of the technologies it studied, if Mr. Currie's analysis of past work from S&T is correct.

So, I certainly hope that those discussions will happen very, very quickly. We look forward to your near-term goals being set as well as future goals.

With that, my time is up and I would turn it over to Ranking Member Payne for 5 minutes.

Mr. PAYNE. Yes, thank you, Madam Chairwoman. I was going to mention that Dr. Brothers, I am concerned that you haven't been able to straighten all this out in 6 weeks.

[Laughter.]

Just to that point.

But Under Secretary Cummiskey, I am concerned that the Department did not engage in a thorough Analysis of Alternatives until the acquisition of Gen–3 was well underway. I am glad that it has suspended the acquisition to reevaluate when GAO raised the red flags in 2012.

Can you tell the subcommittee how much money has been appropriated to Gen–3 and how much of the funding that has already been obligated and what the Department plans to do with the funds appropriated to Gen–3 that have not already been obligated?

Mr. CUMMISKEY. Thank you, Ranking Member Payne.

With regard to the expenditures, I checked with the CFO's office. The amount that has been spent on Generation–3 since 2009 is $61 million. Of that, it was spent primarily on evaluation and testing capabilities. There was some money spent prior to 2009 on other aspects of BioWatch. But as to the question of Gen–3, it is $61 million.

Mr. PAYNE. Okay. And the dollars for Gen–3 that haven't been obligated?

Mr. CUMMISKEY. There were $16 million that were unspent as part of the appropriations and were routed to the Treasury.

Mr. PAYNE. Back to Treasury?

Mr. CUMMISKEY. Yes.

Mr. PAYNE. Okay. All right. Let's see. Also, this is a little bit off-topic, but since I have a captive audience I will take the opportunity.

As you know, I have introduced legislation to resolve inter-operability communication problems within DHS, first identified by the inspector general in November 2012.

This legislation is H.R. 4289 and will be marked up by the full committee tomorrow, as a matter of fact.

Have you seen this or reviewed this legislation? Can I count on you to work with me to address this important issue? Because any time I am involved in crafting legislation, I try to get as many people involved to help it be good legislation, so when it is finally presented all sides have had an opportunity to weigh in on it.

Your thoughts?

Mr. CUMMISKEY. Sure. Congressman, I had an opportunity to review 4289 last evening. Just on a personal note as a former State Senator who spent a lot of time on inter-operability issues, I really applaud and appreciate your efforts. We look forward to working with you to advance what is really an essential role for the Department.

Mr. PAYNE. Absolutely. I mean, based on the information that I have learned and gathered since coming to this committee and the Congress that the whole question around inter-operability throughout agencies and to the States and locals is crucial in order for continuity in addressing the safety of the homeland.

So I thank you for that.

Also, it seems that one of the problems—okay. Never mind.

Dr. Brinsfield, the BioWatch is currently deployed in 30 cities. Under Gen–3 the program was expanded to 50 cities. What was the rationale behind expanding the program to 50 cities, and was it based on specific intelligence suggested that such an expansion was necessary?

Dr. BRINSFIELD. Sir, when the program was proposed to be expanded, it was working off lists provided by the FEMA grants initiative as to cities that would be possibly at risk and covered under that program.

That list has since been moved back.

Mr. PAYNE. Okay, so expanding to the 50 cities is not a priority or will it continue to be a priority?

Dr. BRINSFIELD. Sir, we don't currently have funding to expand in that area.

Mr. PAYNE. Okay.

Okay, Madam Chairwoman. I yield back. Thank you.

Mrs. BROOKS. Thank you.

With respect to—because it sounds as if the current system, Gen–2 is going to be in place for some time with no really new systems having been identified on the horizon or certainly submitted in any budget request, speaking of funding, which might also be, in part, because the administration has yet to produce the plan. But with that said and to ensure that Gen–2, the GAO do make any recommendations with respect to improvements to Gen–2, Mr. Currie?

Mr. CURRIE. No, ma'am. Actually, most of our focus has been on the Gen–3 acquisition——

Mrs. BROOKS. Do you have any recommendations for Gen–2 at this point? Are you prepared to make any recommendations with respect to Gen–2, which is what we have in 30 cities?

Mr. CURRIE. Currently, we have work on-going looking at the technical capabilities of Gen–2, which may result in recommendations. But at this point, we don't have any specific reported recommendations. As I laid out in my testimony, we have many questions and concerns about what is going to happen with the program, but this has all happened so recently that it is very unclear what is going to transpire at this point.

Mrs. BROOKS. Dr. Disraelly, do you have any recommendations with respect to the current system improvements?

Mr. CURRIE. No, ma'am. That was outside the scope of our study.

Mrs. BROOKS. Okay. So, Dr. Brinsfield, Dr. Brothers, and I do appreciate our recent visit to the NBIC, which was very enlightening and I want to thank you and your staff for putting on a very—you know, a wonderful presentation about NBIC. But what improvements might you have or suggestions that should be made to the Gen–2 system, in order to make it the most efficient and best system, if that is what we have got right now?

Dr. BRINSFIELD. Thank you, ma'am, and Mr. Payne for your visits. We greatly appreciated you coming to the NBIC. We are looking at a number of issues that we will be coordinating with Dr. Brothers staff as well. Some of them are about how we collect the samples. Some of them are about the form that the samples are collected in, so that might provide more information. Some of them are about giving us a warning, if something might have been released early so that we could go and take a look at the sample earlier.

All those—there are about seven of those different potential incremental improvements to the current system and we are looking at them as we speak to see which we could field in the near-near-term. By that I mean, within the year or so and others that we might be able to implement in the near-term.

Mrs. BROOKS. Might you be considering detectors and use by other Federal agencies as well to supplement the current Gen–2 system?

Dr. BRINSFIELD. There are different types of detectors that we have looked at in different Federal agencies. As you know, we have looked at studies done by a number of different groups to look at what is currently in place and using the technology readiness levels, you know, what could be fielded now. There isn't a start-to-finish detector in another agency that would be better than our current system. So that is where we are at looking at improvements to the current system.

Mrs. BROOKS. Dr. Brothers, I do appreciate that you would only been there 6 weeks. But in your—and having been in new positions in the past in kind of order of priority, where does the Gen–2 and the BioWatch program, you know, fall in S&T?

Mr. BROTHERS. You understand, it is clear to me the importance of this capability, the threat that bio poses to the country. You know, right now about 25 percent of our budget is spent in chembio. So I think just based on that alone, you can see, it is a large priority for us.

So yes, it is important. I think it is also to consider the near-term. I think the comment came up earlier about, you know, how this is used. I think, you know, taking a system-to-system approach both near-term and far-term is important.

Mrs. BROOKS. Dr. Brinsfield, can you share with us briefly, how is BioWatch and NBIC working together?

Dr. BRINSFIELD. Yes, ma'am.

I know we discussed this when you came to visit and for us, it is a high priority to make sure that the two are working together.

BioWatch is a tool, a very useful tool that gives us a data-point in which we can look at to see if there has been a biological event. NBIC or the National Biosurveillance Integration Center looks at this from the continuum, from early through, with the departments and agencies collecting all information available.

It is our role in this next bit of time to see how we can make the two, use the two more efficiently to work together. We already use the two on a daily basis to provide information to both States and locals to the White House and we are looking at how we can sort of institutionalize that coordination.

Mrs. BROOKS. Didn't you indicate at that time that the personnel over—with responsibility for BioWatch were moving to NBIC's site?

Dr. BRINSFIELD. Yes, ma'am.

One of the ways we are going to work on that collaboration issue is to make sure that all personnel are housed in the same area so they can have those day-to-day conversations more easily.

Mrs. BROOKS. Then also can you—the current BioWatch detectors that are currently deployed, how is that information provided to NBIC so that it can be disseminated to State and local authorities?

How does that work from the BioWatch collection to NBIC to State and locals?

Dr. BRINSFIELD. So speaking to the BioWatch CONOPS as was previously mentioned, there is a way that the States, locals, Federal agencies, all of which have a role, including NBIC and NBIC's partners, can participate in an information call when you have positive results from one of the BioWatch.

It is meant to set it up so that you can put it in perspective of what else people are seeing, what is going on and make sort-of a collaborative decision on the path forward. That process has been in place for a number of years and has been tested numerous times. It is something that we work very hard to make sure we are doing this in collaboration all the way through our health and human services partners, USDA and others back to the field and States and locals.

Mrs. BROOKS. Thank you.

My time is now up—for 5 minutes of questioning from the Ranking Member. Okay.

If I might have one moment, please?

At this time, we have no further questions.

I do want to thank all of the witnesses for their valuable testimony, both that was written and your answers to our questions today.

Members of the subcommittee may have some additional questions for the witnesses. We will ask you to respond to those in writing.

I just would like to close by reiterating as I began, the importance of the administration providing the implementation plan for the National Biosurveillance Strategy.

Additionally, it is very difficult. Congress wants to be a strong partner in ensuring that our country is safe from bioterrorism threats and I believe that from this committee, in a bipartisan way, we are very concerned that we don't have the plan from the administration forward.

We are in the dark as to what the administration wants funded and what the needs are in the country. We don't believe that the threat is diminishing around the world and we look forward to receiving those plans and also look forward to continuing discussions in the Classified manner in which you suggested.

So at this time, pursuant to committee rule 7(e), the hearing record will be open for 10 days.

Without objection, the subcommittee stands adjourned.

Thank you.

[Whereupon, at 11:20 a.m., the subcommittee was adjourned.]

APPENDIX

QUESTIONS FROM CHAIRWOMAN SUSAN W. BROOKS FOR KATHRYN BRINSFIELD AND REGINALD BROTHERS

Question 1a. On November 22 of last year, several Members of the committee wrote a letter to DHS to ask about progress made in looking at the coordination of programs and activities with Weapons of Mass Destruction, Chemical, Biological, Radiological, and Nuclear responsibilities. This letter cited the fiscal year 2013 DHS appropriations bill report language that requested DHS to submit a consolidation plan to merge the Domestic Nuclear Detection Office (DNDO) and the Office of Health Affairs (OHA). We received a response from Secretary Johnson stating that "I have directed my staff to begin working on several initial focus areas that are intended to build organizational capacity in support of our primary objective: the effective and efficient execution of our mission."

Can you please provide us an update on that progress?

Answer. The Department of Homeland Security (DHS) continues to explore alternatives to re-orient and re-invigorate several headquarters functions and organizations to meet the intent of the Secretary's Unity of Effort initiative and its ultimate objective: Empowering DHS components to effectively execute their operations. Science and Technology (S&T), OHA, DNDO, and the rest of the Department have been working together closely to analyze a range of possibilities for closer coordination of chemical, biological, radiological, and nuclear (CBRN) responsibilities. DHS is considering a number of viable options, but we are not prepared to suggest one particular path forward at this time.

Question 1b. Do you believe that the Weapons of Mass Destruction (WMD) functions of DHS would be better consolidated than in separate offices?

Answer. There are advantages and disadvantages to both options, and those will be articulated to the Secretary to inform his decision on organizational changes. In the mean time, the offices with WMD responsibilities will continue to coordinate closely on matters of mutual interest, whether related to policy, budget, acquisition, plans, or operations.

Question 2a. Your testimony refers to the business model used by the BioWatch program. This model, as you described it, uses the BioWatch units that are provided by the Federal Government and then "a network of local, State, and Federal laboratories." Much focus has been placed on the acquisition and technology of BioWatch but I am also interested in hearing about challenges in using this type of approach.

Do you think that this model still works today?

Question 2b. What challenges exist in using this model?

Question 2c. Do you plan on looking at alternatives to this model moving forward?

Answer. BioWatch is a tool of the public health and first/emergency response communities. The network of local, State, and Federal laboratories and stakeholders is an essential element of the program. These partnerships include public health, emergency management, first responders, law enforcement, and laboratory officials. This model has proven to be a successful integration of a Federal program operating at a State/local level that allows all partners access to the information and tools they need to make informed and timely decisions, while staying consistent with local response operations. We work in partnership with transit agencies, local police departments, health departments, etc. to build effective networks within each jurisdiction. The communications and exercises conducted with these networks through the BioWatch program build personal and professional relationships within this community and improve the ability at all levels of government to respond to a large-scale bioterrorism attack. Each jurisdiction has a multi-agency group that coordinates the implementation, routine operations, and enhancement of their jurisdictional BioWatch program. Recent reductions in State and local funding have led to challenges for public health departments, who have to carefully balance their resources among competing priorities, and have prevented some communities currently outside the network from joining the program. Additionally, each jurisdiction has specific needs and protocols that make it difficult to adopt a standardized approach across the entire BioWatch network.

Potential technology changes may alter the current program processes. In cooperation with S&T, the BioWatch program is examining as a near-term strategy several technology approaches which essentially keep the current collector-laboratory approach, but upgrade the technology used in aerosol collection, the laboratory identification methods, or both. Any improvements would be predicated on efficiency, timeliness, and cost considerations. As longer-term alternatives are developed, alterations to the current model may be considered that would be contingent on improving efficiency, timeliness, and/or decreasing costs before being deployed.

Question 3a. As you work to identify and develop alternatives to the Gen–2 system, and appreciating the critical role technology providers in industry can play in advancing this technology, what are you doing to communicate with the private sector regarding the way ahead for the advancement of detection systems so they can participate in this effort?

Answer. Any new acquisition of technology will be conducted in accordance with the DHS Acquisition Management Directive 102–01 (MD 102–01) acquisition process to emphasize transparent, full, and open competition. The BioWatch program has discussed potential technology approaches with the commercial sector and has met with industry representatives, when appropriate, to discuss needs and available technologies for potential implementation. Potential Gen–2 enhancement efforts will largely be executed through traditional acquisition instruments such as Requests for Information, Broad Agency Announcements (BAAs), and scheduled "Industry Days" that allow direct discussion of BioWatch technical needs with multiple industry representatives. As one example, S&T's recently initiated investigation of detection networking architectures began with an Industry Day to allow discussion of concepts with industry, and a BAA-enabled industry to describe concepts for funding consideration. In addition to these traditional mechanisms, S&T looks forward to taking advantage of its newly-delegated prize authority to engage and harvest performers through a potential biosurveillance grand challenge.

Under the new leadership of Dr. Brothers, a priority for S&T has been finding more effective ways to harness the energy and expertise of the Homeland Security Industrial Base. Working better with industry is essential to developing near- and long-term solutions to homeland security problems. Part of this effort over the last 2 months has involved development of a homeland security science and technology strategic document that lays out visionary near- and long-term Research and Development (R&D) goals that will, among other purposes, serve as hooks for engaging industry. The strategy is also supported by on-going development of technology road maps by S&T's research divisions in S&T's major investment areas. When completed, the strategy and road maps will be valuable tools for communicating S&T's investments and vision, including where perceived gaps and opportunities may lie, and driving complementary investment by industry stakeholders.

Question 3b. How are you communicating with State and local officials to discuss their needs going forward?

Answer. The BioWatch Program is communicating with State and local partners on the status of technology upgrades within BioWatch and working with them to assess their needs through a number of channels. These include webinars and program updates to inform all BioWatch jurisdictions as well as Federal partners of the current status of the BioWatch program and the cancellation of the Gen–3 acquisition. Daily interactions by the jurisdictional coordinators who serve as liaisons in each BioWatch Jurisdiction and the implementation of new technologies under consideration will be discussed at length as part of the National BioWatch Workshop in October 2014. In addition, the BioWatch program staff attend and discuss needs with BioWatch Advisory Committees (BACs are multi-agency groups that coordinate the implementation, routine operations, and enhancement of their jurisdictional BioWatch program) during regularly-scheduled BAC meetings throughout the year and will also discuss jurisdictional needs while attending exercises held within the BioWatch jurisdictions. The BioWatch program has also requested input from local laboratory and public health representatives on the selection criteria used to inform the evaluation of laboratory instrumentation to ensure end-user needs are being met. The contact information of the BioWatch Program and Deputy Program Manager are well-advertised, and all members of BioWatch operations at all levels of government have been encouraged to call and discuss their needs and concerns directly with Program leadership.

Question 4. A 2008 National Center for Risk and Economic Analysis of Terrorism Events report estimated the impact of a bioterror attack on a major league sports stadium would cost between $62 and $73 billion. In light of this estimate and the

Gen–3 cancellation, how does the Department plan to address this threat? Has the Post-Implementation Plan been completed? If not, what is the time line for its completion?

Answer. OHA concurs with the severity of the estimate offered by CREATE. Further, BioWatch has consulted independent research within the scientific community that validates the significance and severity of such an event.

The operational BioWatch system will continue its normal operations as a fundamental part of the Nation's biodefense. Moving forward, OHA and S&T are working closely on development of a systems approach to next-generation biodetection including joint development of requirements. The systems approach will also look carefully at the results of an evaluation, completed by the BioWatch program earlier this year, of the existing operational BioWatch system. As the path forward is finalized, a full range of potential investments will be under consideration from near-term incremental improvements to longer-term shifts to a distributed, networked, sensor-agnostic biosurveillance architecture with potential for capability beyond what the Department initially envisioned for Gen–3.

The Post-Implementation Review along with its accompanying briefing is currently under DHS review.

QUESTIONS FROM CHAIRWOMAN SUSAN W. BROOKS FOR KATHRYN BRINSFIELD

Question 1. Dr. Polk testified before this subcommittee in April 2012 that OHA and the CDC were in the process of developing a pilot program for the voluntary, pre-event vaccination of first responders. However, more than 2 years later, little progress has been made.

What is the status of this important pilot program to protect our protectors?

Answer. The Department of Homeland Security (DHS), in coordination with the Centers for Disease Control and Prevention (CDC), is developing the Anthrax preparedness and Protection Pilot to provide responders with a voluntary and comprehensive approach for preparing and protecting themselves consistent with broader anthrax preparedness guidance. Enhancing the ability of our Nation's responders to conduct life-saving activities more safely and efficiently is a goal of this Department, as responders face a number of real and potential threats, including anthrax.

DHS's Office of Health Affairs (OHA) has been assessing the demand for and acceptance of pre-event anthrax vaccination for responders through a proposed Anthrax Preparedness and Protection Pilot. The goal of such a pilot is to assess the demand by responders and communities for the anthrax vaccine and the capability of Federal, State, local, Tribal, and territorial governments and organizations to deliver this program with the ultimate goal of better protecting responders and communities.

Past biodefense vaccine efforts, such as the 2003 effort to encourage vaccination of health care workers and first responders against smallpox, encountered challenges in meeting the needs of the response community. Actively engaging the responder and public health communities will be the backbone on which this effort will be built. OHA has conducted outreach activities with 243 individuals representing public health, occupational health, emergency management, and responder communities and has increased awareness among many more stakeholders. Through this effort, stakeholders have expressed concerns such as their need to have increased awareness of the threat, education about comprehensive personal health protection, vaccine safety, liability protection, logistical implementation, and a strategic plan to protect unvaccinated families and communities. DHS and the CDC have redefined core program elements which are responsive to stakeholder requirements and are critical as we consider actions to the design and build-out pilot promotion and coordination of this effort. OHA is actively conferring with partners both inside and outside of the Department to capitalize on existing programs to implement this pilot. As pilot elements are developed, DHS will solicit community applications for two States to participate in the pilot through the Federal Register, making the process both open and transparent process. Successful applicants will be well-positioned to deliver a safe and quality program through demonstration of a qualified occupational health and safety program, accessible education platforms and the necessary infrastructure to handle the complete chain of receipt through delivery and monitoring of recipients of the vaccine.

Question 2. In addition to reducing detection time, one of the goals of Gen–3 was to increase indoor detection. With the cancellation of Gen–3, what is the plan now for indoor detection?

Answer. The technology currently used in BioWatch is employed indoors in limited locations; however its use requires multiple sampling events that increase costs to the Program. OHA, in cooperation with S&T, is examining a number of alternative approaches to improve indoor detection including, but not limited to, the use of air monitoring systems that continuously sample indoor air spaces for irregularities (unusually high particle counts, fluorescence signatures, etc.) and provide a warning within minutes of a suspicious aerosol event to trigger and direct response, upgrading collectors using a collection medium that is able to preserve the viability of the collected organisms (e.g., liquid-based), and portable identification technology that allows for the rapid field identification of potential agents. Through S&T, DHS is also investigating alternative architectures for networked systems of sensors equipped with analytic capability for rapid determination of unusual and potentially hazardous biological and chemical contamination in the air, both for indoor and outdoor environments.

Question 3. The value and effectiveness of BioWatch early detection is premised on the capability of State and local public health authorities to respond, for example, by directing the mass dispensing of medications or establishing mass treatment centers. Without the capability to respond with an appropriate public health and medical measures to minimize illness and death, the BioWatch warning will not produce a benefit.

Please discuss what actions DHS takes (in partnership with the appropriate Federal, State, and local authorities) to ensure that sufficient medical countermeasures are in place to respond to an attack with any of the agents Gen–2 is designed.

Answer. The BioWatch program not only provides the critical first laboratory detection of an aerosolized threat, it also supports the infrastructure that coordinates the initial awareness for response officials, including within the medical and public health community, that will initiate protective actions such as dispensing medical countermeasures (MCMs). The BioWatch Exercise Program provides BioWatch jurisdictions up to 7 exercises per year to improve local, State, and Federal preparedness for a large-scale bioterrorism attack. These exercises are tailored to each jurisdiction's needs, are multi-disciplinary in nature, provide specific subject-matter expertise as needed, and are tightly focused on the initial BioWatch Actionable Result (BAR) assessment phase. In each jurisdiction, the BioWatch program has formalized partnerships with local and State agencies that include public health officials, emergency management, first responders, law enforcement, and laboratory officials. These local and State officials have designated points of contact at Federal agencies to aid in coordination.

The Department of Health and Human Services (HHS) manages the Strategic National Stockpile (SNS) of MCMs as well as the Cities Readiness Initiative (CRI). Through CRI, State and large metropolitan public health departments have developed plans to respond to a large-scale bioterrorist event by dispensing antibiotics to the entire population of an identified metropolitan statistical area within 48 hours. Further, Executive Order (EO) 13527 (December 20, 2009), "Establishing Federal Capability for the Timely Provision of Medical Countermeasures Following a Biological Attack," Section 3, explicitly calls for the Secretaries of Homeland Security, Health and Human Services, and Defense, along with the Attorney General, to develop a Federal capability to immediately supplement the capabilities of affected jurisdictions to rapidly distribute MCM following a biological attack. On September 9, 2010, the Secretaries of the Departments of Homeland Security (DHS) and Health and Human Services (HHS), endorsed and forwarded to the White House National Security Staff, The Federal Interagency Concept of Operational Plan-Rapid Medical Countermeasures Dispensing (FICOP–MCM). The FICOP–MCM delineates options for the rapid and coordinated deployment of Federal resources to supplement State and local governments' abilities to dispense MCM. This Federal capability resource is intended to be an initial rapid response to stabilize the situation in partnership with State and local authorities.

FEMA is supporting this regional MCM planning initiative in concert with local CRI planning supported by the Centers for Disease Control and Prevention (CDC). This joint effort includes HHS regional representation; the CDC SNS senior official; as well as appropriate State, county, and city public health and emergency management officials. This initiative will result in a Regional MCM support annex to the Regions' All Hazards Plan that is consistent with the scope, mission essential tasks, and concept of operations outlined in the FICOP–MCM. Each Regional MCM annex will, in turn, describe the Federal supporting concept of operations to support and complement the local CRI plan of the metropolitan area.

Efficient delivery of medical countermeasures requires that critical decisions affecting how MCMs are dispensed be determined before we face such an incident. Towards this goal, DHS has worked with Federal partners, to include CDC, on guidance documents such as prioritization for anthrax vaccine in affected communities that addresses the need of those most at risk as well as the response community that we will rely on in such an incident. To further enable a rapid response, DHS and its partners issued "Guidance for Protecting Responders' Health During the First Week Following A Wide-Area Aerosol Anthrax Attack."

QUESTIONS FROM CHAIRWOMAN SUSAN W. BROOKS FOR CHRIS CUMMISKEY

Question 1. Setting requirements for large-scale acquisitions has been a challenge for the Department since its inception.

What are you doing to work with program offices to ensure that well-developed requirements are put in place prior to the start of an acquisition?

Answer. One of the principal focus areas of Secretary Johnson's *Unity of Effort* initiative, as outlined in his April 22, 2014, memorandum entitled, "Strengthening Departmental Unity of Effort" is to continue to refine our acquisition oversight framework, especially in the earliest stages where acquisition requirements are developed. As part of this initiative, a component-composed and component-chaired *Joint Requirements Council (JRC)* has been established to review cross-component requirements and develop recommendations for investment, as well as changes to training, organization, and operational processes and procedures. The Department continues to enhance its acquisition governance and oversight structures to support and oversee programs after requirements are reviewed and approved by the JRC and DHS leadership. Additionally, the Department, working with its components, has in recent years established robust training and certification programs at the Homeland Security Acquisition Institute for program managers, systems engineers, cost estimators, and contracting specialists. Combined, these efforts will enable components to thoroughly develop organizational requirements on which acquisitions programs may be established.

Question 2. DHS reported to Congress that the original life-cycle cost estimate for the 2009 decision—a point estimate unadjusted for risk—was $2.1 billion. Two years later, in 2011, DHS estimated that Gen–3 was expected to cost $5.8 billion (80 percent confidence) from fiscal year 2012 through June 2028.

What specific steps does DHS plan to take to control costs and provide accurate reports to Congress that accurately describe the life-cycle costs of any follow-on systems or upgrades to Gen–2?

Answer. Over the past 5 years, we have improved acquisition oversight, ensuring full consideration of the investment life cycle in cost estimates. Before any follow-on systems or upgrades to Gen–2, the current operationally-deployed system, are approved to proceed, they must get Acquisition Review Board approval, which includes full review and approval of planned life-cycle costs.

As the Department's Science and Technology Directorate, in partnership with OHA, explores the capability gaps and the capability needs of automated aerosol biodetection capabilities, any proposed follow-on systems or upgrades to Gen–2 will be under the management practices of the Department's acquisition oversight policy, Management Directive 102–01. This management process controls the cost of acquisition programs in two ways. First, programs are required to develop accurate, credible, comprehensive, and well-documented Life-Cycle Cost Estimates at major acquisition decision event milestones to ensure that the costs are accurate for the life cycle of the program. Second, any future follow-on systems or upgrades to BioWatch Gen–2 are required by the DHS Chief Financial Officer to have met affordability requirements before proceeding through acquisition phases.

Question 3. Will DHS continue to use the 80 percent confidence factor to ensure Congress has more reliable cost estimates in the future?

Answer. While DHS policy requires acquisition programs be resourced to at least a 50% confidence level of the cost estimate, estimates are conducted at each confidence interval, and the ARB then discusses the appropriate estimate to use for budgeting based on the investment and program risk.

○

www.ingramcontent.com/pod-product-compliance
Lightning Source LLC
Chambersburg PA
CBHW080539290526
45790CB00006B/2469